The SCIENTIFIC AMERICAN
Day in the Life
of Your Brain

SCIENTIFIC AMERICAN

SCIENTIFIC AMERICAN

MIND

BEHAVIOR · BRAIN SCIENCE · INSIGHTS

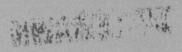

The SCIENTIFIC AMERICAN

Day in the Life of Your Brain

JUDITH HORSTMAN

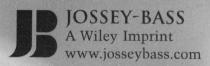

JOSSEY-BASS
A Wiley Imprint
www.josseybass.com

Published by Jossey-Bass
A Wiley Imprint
989 Market Street, San Francisco, CA 94103-1741—www.josseybass.com

Jossey-Bass books and products are available through most bookstores. To contact Jossey-Bass directly call our Customer Care Department within the U.S. at 800-956-7739, outside the U.S. at 317-572-3986, or fax 317-572-4002.

Jossey-Bass also publishes its books in a variety of electronic formats. Some content that appears in print may not be available in electronic books.

Library of Congress Cataloging-in-Publication Data
The Scientific American day in the life of your brain / Judith Horstman.—1st ed.
   p. cm.
  Includes bibliographical references and index.
  ISBN 978-0-470-37623-2 (cloth)
  1. Neurosciences. 2. Brain. 3. Human behavior. 4. Body and mind. I. Horstman, Judith.
II. Scientific American, inc. III. Title: Day in the life of your brain.
  RC341.S346 2009
  616.8—dc22   2009013923

Printed in the United States of America
FIRST EDITION
HB Printing   10 9 8 7 6 5 4 3

Contents

For my beautiful and brainy grandchildren:
Isabela, Ragsdale Blue, Raj, and Raina Leela (Lulu)

Acknowledgments

This book would not have been possible without the research and the articles of the many excellent contributors of *Scientific American* and *Scientific American Mind:* their work is in large part the basis of this book and is acknowledged in detail in the Sources. Thanks to the staff at *Scientific American*—Diane McGarvey, director of ancillary products, and Linda Hertz, manager of permissions and rights—for help with the many editorial details involved in processing hundreds of articles from the archives. The Jossey-Bass team provided invaluable support: thanks to publisher Paul Foster, who originated the concept for this book, marketing manager Jennifer Wenzel, production manager Carol Hartland, copywriter Karen Warner, and copyeditor Beverly Miller. Special thanks to executive editor Alan Rinzler and senior editorial assistant Nana Twumasi. I am grateful to several scientists who gave this text a careful read and some thoughtful commentary, especially Merrill M. Mitler, program director at the National Institute of Neurological Disorders and Stroke, Kelly A. Dakin, a doctoral candidate in the Program in Neuroscience at Harvard University/Harvard Medical School, and Jason Coleman, a Howard Hughes Medical Institute postdoctoral fellow at the Picower Institute for Learning and Memory at MIT. Many thanks also to literary agent Andrea Hurst, author and editor Jennifer Basye Sander of Write By the Lake, and my many fellow writers, including Ann Crew, Joan Aragone, and the Writers Who Wine (you know who you are) for their support and encouragement.

Preface

What's your brain doing right now? What was it doing when you woke up, got hungry, went to work, danced, made love, got angry, got happy, dreamed, and fell asleep? How in the world does your brain recognize people and places, and how does it make decisions and memories? What is happening in your brain as you go through a typical day and night?

These questions (and more) were the spark for this book: an hour-by-hour journal of a day in the life of your brain and how it affects you as you go about your day. The editors at Jossey-Bass conceived the idea and took it to *Scientific American* magazine, a treasure trove of fine articles about these very issues.

I was brought to the project to weave it together from the *Scientific American* articles, editing, restructuring, and adding materials to give a daily progression that most of us can recognize in our own lives.

It was a pleasure to delve into the excellent articles in the *Scientific American* archives, and hard not to get lost in all of the fascinating material. I found many surprises, recognized many processes in my own brain, and was left with even more respect than ever for this three pounds of "thinking meat."

The book is structured by the clock, beginning at 5:00 A.M. as we (or some of us) awake, and ending at 4:00 A.M., in the last moments of sleep. You might find yourself comparing the activities of your own brain as you read.

As scientists continue to study the brain, we'll know even more about how our brain works and influences us moment to moment. We'll also know more about how to control it. Meanwhile, this book represents the fascinating and entertaining state-of-the-art brain science that we can use in our daily lives.

JUDITH HORSTMAN

The SCIENTIFIC AMERICAN
Day in the Life
of Your Brain

Introduction

Your brain is the most important organ in your body. Without it, nothing else would work—and you wouldn't be aware of it if it did.

It's the repository of memory, mind, and feeling; the conductor of the orchestra that's your body; the seat of consciousness that is you.

Every day this three pounds of "thinking meat" navigates you through the ordinary and extraordinary events of being human—from waking to sleep, and everything in between. It guides your body through motions of intricacy and delicacy, ranging from the most gross to the most subtle of movements, emotions, and thoughts; from unconsciousness to wide awake and even hyperawareness. It allows you to see the stars through a telescope and a molecule in a microscope—and using instruments the brain has created.

Until recently, most of what we know about how the brain works came from examining damaged brains, where scientists learned what was lost, or by studying animal brains (it is, after all, unethical and illegal to cut up living humans).

Today specialized imaging techniques and instruments have given us new windows into the living brain, thanks to volunteers, from meditating monks to copulating couples, who agree to have their brains imaged in action. Using instruments such as functional magnetic resonance imaging (fMRI) to view the brain as thoughts, feelings, and actions occur, researchers are able to see which parts are activated when we have sex, eat, express anger, listen to music, dance, sleep, or meditate.

There have been many surprises.

Your brain, for example, is more like a Rube Goldberg contraption than the computer to which it is so often compared. It's jam-packed with functions, programs, connections, and interconnections that often overlap with each other. That's probably because its many complex and diverse parts evolved over time, piggybacked in ways that intertwine and are still not completely understood.

And it's even less like the old phrenology models of a human head, with their neatly color-coded brain compartments. In fact, your brain is not even like the basic texts on brain science of a few decades ago.

Processes thought to be hardwired are turning out to be adaptable. The brain is not as set in stone as previously thought. We are finding that the same neurotransmitters and brain regions that foster love, cooperation, and trust also foster lust, addiction, and fear. Sex, drugs, and rock and roll have the same address. Memory is handled by several different parts of the brain and seems to do much of its short-term work while we sleep. Music plays in many parts of the brain. And when push comes to shove, your most primitive emotional brain part, the amygdala, rules. There are many more connections from the amygdala to the thinking brain than the other way around.

Most exciting is the finding that your brain is teaching old neurons new tricks and even making new neurons. When some sections of the brain go dark, other parts of the brain can learn to take over part of those functions. In fact, many who have half their brain removed for medical reasons function pretty well with just one hemisphere. See "Do You Need Only Half a Brain?" page 7.

A caveat: although we title this book *A Day in the Life of Your Brain*, it cannot be so. Your brain is unique and uniquely yours, affected by your age, genes, race, ethnic and cultural origins, family culture, diet, and even birth order: all the things that make you *you*. However, there are universal processes, and the equipment is basically the same in most of us, except for the extremes of aging and disease and trauma.

DID YOU KNOW . . . ?

- Your brain has an estimated 100 billion neuron cells and 40 quadrillion connections. But nobody knows for sure.
- You used to have even more cells and connections. By the time you were born, you lost half the neurons you had as a fetus. In your teens, you lose even more as your brain streamlines itself for optimal function.
- Your brain is big. With its many creases, folds, and layers, it would take up more than three times its area if it were spread out flat.
- Your brain is an energy hog. Although your brain occupies only 2 percent of your body, it sucks 20 percent of your body energy when you are at rest.
- Your brain can make new neurons. Scientists are discovering the brain makes new connections and creates neurons in some areas to meet new needs, and it does so into old age.
- The brain can change. It can adapt from exterior and interior experiences to take on new functions. The more you repeat something—an action or a thought—the more brain space is dedicated to it. In musicians, for example, the part of the brain that controls fingers used to play an instrument is up to 130 percent larger than that section in the rest of us. While the very young brain is most adaptive, old brains can be retrained as well.
- Your brain prunes itself. Much as a gardener prunes roses, the brain weakens less-used connections and strengthens useful connections, which actually improves memory.
- Stress can shrink your brain—and meditation and exercise strengthen your brain and your ability to relieve stress.
- Your brain's surface itself has no sensation. You could touch it (and surgeons do) and feel nothing. Only when the interior parts are stimulated do you feel, both tactilely and emotionally. This anomaly allows patients to be conscious when doctors perform delicate brain surgeries.

You're probably neither a computer tech nor a brain scientist. What we suspect you want to know is: What's happening in there as you go about your day? Which part does what, how, when, and—if we know—why? The hour-by-hour sections of this book explain what's going on during some of our most ordinary and extraordinary everyday events.

You Gotta Know the Territory: A Short Tour of Your Brain

Your brain is about three pounds of flesh, nerves, and fluid that looks like an oversized walnut but is much softer. Nestled in the protective shell of your bony skull, it has the squiggly consistency of gelatin.

The overall brain is often described in three parts, from the bottom up, just the way your brain evolved over millennia.

The primitive brain—the brain stem or hindbrain—that sits at the top of the spine is the oldest part of your brain. It takes care of basic business such as breathing, heartbeat, digestion, reflexive actions, sleeping, and arousal. It includes the spinal cord, which sends messages from the brain to the rest of the body, and the cerebellum, which coordinates balance and rote motions, like riding a bike or catching a ball.

Above this, the brain is divided into two hemispheres connected by a thick band of fibers and nerves called the corpus callosum. Most brain parts from here on up come in pairs, one in each hemisphere. And although these two halves are very similar, they are not twins. Each side functions slightly differently from the other. In an oft-cited overgeneralization, the right hemisphere is associated with creativity and the left hemisphere with logic. For reasons unknown, the messages between the hemispheres and the rest of our body criss-cross, so that the right brain controls our left side, and vice versa.

Your emotional brain—the inner brain or limbic system—is tucked deep inside the bulk of the midbrain and acts as the gatekeeper between the spinal cord and the thinking brain in the cerebrum above. It regulates sex hormones, sleep cycles, hunger, emotions, and addictions.

The amygdala handles survival needs and emotions such as fear and anger. It's responsible for the fight-or-flight reaction. The tiny

WHY DOES YOUR BRAIN USE SO MUCH POWER?

Your brain is an energy hog. It takes up 2 percent of your real estate, but uses 20 percent of the body's total energy haul when you are at rest—more energy than any other human organ. That's probably because your brain never seems to rest.

Scientists believe it uses the bulk of that energy—two-thirds of it—to fuel the electrical impulses neurons use to "fire" or send signals to communicate with one another. A study in the *Proceedings of the National Academy of Sciences* suggests that your brain uses the remaining third for "housekeeping," or cell health maintenance.

Housekeeping is important for keeping brain tissue alive and well, and for the many biological and chemical exchanges processed in the brain. Charged sodium, calcium, and potassium atoms (or ions) are continuously passed through the membranes of cells so that neurons can recharge to fire. Adenosine triphosphate (ATP) supplies the energy required for these ions to traverse cell membranes. When researchers measured the brain level of ATP in rats, they found the more alert animals used more of this substance. When the lab rats were knocked out, they produced 50 percent fewer ATP molecules than when they were mildly anesthetized. That ATP seems to go mostly toward cell maintenance, scientists believe.

hippocampus is the gatekeeper for short-term memories, and the hypothalamus controls your biological clock and hormone balance. The thalamus passes along sensory information to and from the cerebrum, the limbic system, and the spinal cord. The basal ganglia surrounds the thalamus and is responsible for voluntary movement. The so-called pleasure center or reward circuit is also based in the limbic system, involving the nucleus accumbens and ventral tegmental area.

At the very top of the brain is the wrinkly and crevassed cerebrum—the part we usually see when we picture a brain and what is sometimes called "the crown jewel" of the body. The actual crown is the nickel-thin layer of the cerebral cortex (or neocortex) that covers the cerebrum. This is the most recently evolved part of the brain—the part, some say, that makes us human. It controls thoughts, reasoning, language, planning, and imagination.

The cerebrum has four major sections or lobes. Research has found that the frontal lobes take care of speech, movement commands, and reasoning. The occipital lobes in the back take care of vision, while the temporal lobes (above your ears) are responsible for hearing and for understanding speech and appreciating music. The parietal lobes run across the top and sides of the brain and are the primary sensory areas, receiving information about taste, temperature, touch, and movement. They are also involved in reading and math.

But your brain is more than geography. It's chemistry and electricity as well.

All of these parts are made up of nerve cells called neurons that carry information throughout your body. Some neurons are three feet long, and most of them live as long as you do (in contrast to other cells that die and are renewed). These neurons are separated by microscopically tiny gaps called synapses. Each neuron can communicate with hundreds of thousands of other neurons by releasing neurotransmitters—chemicals to carry messages over the synaptic gap—or by a minute electrical impulse. Billions of tiny blood vessels (capillaries) feed your brain, carrying oxygen, glucose, nutrients, and hormones to brain cells so they can do their work.

Your Neurotransmitters

There are more than a hundred different neurotransmitters, with more being discovered. Scientists are finding that many hormones can play the role of neurotransmitter as well. Here are some of the neurotransmitters your brain uses every day:

- Acetylcholine gets us going: it excites cells, activates muscles, and is involved in wakefulness, attentiveness, anger, aggression, and sexuality. Alzheimer's disease is associated with a shortage of acetylcholine.

DO YOU NEED ONLY HALF A BRAIN?

A surgery that removes half the brain is a drastic solution for disorders that can't be controlled any other way. Brain surgeons have performed hemispherectomies on patients who undergo dozens of debilitating seizures daily that primarily afflict one hemisphere and resist all medication and treatments. Left untreated, these disorders can damage the rest of the brain.

Surprisingly, this surgery usually has no apparent effect on personality or memory. Does that mean a person needs only half a brain? Yes and no. People can survive and function pretty well after the procedure, but they will have some physical disabilities. The body parts that are affected depend on the person's age at the time of the surgery. For adults, there can be significant loss of function on one side of the body and some vision impairment. If the left side of the brain is taken out, most people have problems with their speech.

The younger a person is when having the hemispherectomy, the less likely there is to be speech disability. Neurosurgeons have performed the functional operation on children as young as three months old. In these tiny patients, memory and personality develop normally.

A study of 111 children who underwent the procedure at Johns Hopkins between 1975 and 2001 found that 86 percent are either seizure free or have nondisabling seizures that don't require medication. Another study found that children who underwent a hemispherectomy often improved academically once their seizures stopped. One became champion bowler of her class, one was chess champion of his state, and others are in college doing very nicely.

Researchers are probing how the remaining cerebral hemispheres acquire language, sensory, motor, and other functions, which could shed a great deal of light on the brain's ability to adapt.

- Glutamate is a major excitatory neurotransmitter, dispersed widely throughout the brain. It's involved in learning and memory.
- GABA (gamma-aminobutyric acid) slows everything down and helps keep your system in balance. It helps regulate anxiety.
- Endorphins act as hormones and neurotransmitters: they reduce pain sensations and increase pleasure. The name, by the way, is a combination of *end(ogenous) (m)orphine.*
- Epinephrine, also called adrenaline, keeps you alert and your blood pressure balanced, and it jumps in when you need energy. It's produced and released by the adrenal glands in times of stress. Too much can increase anxiety or tension. Norepinephrine (noradrenaline) is a precursor and has similar actions.
- Dopamine is vital for voluntary movement, attentiveness, motivation, and pleasure. It's a key player in addiction.
- Serotonin helps regulate body temperature, memory, emotion, sleep, appetite, and mood. Many antidepressants work by regulating serotonin.
- Oxytocin is both a hormone and a neurotransmitter. It's responsible for labor, breast milk, mother love, and romantic love and trust.

Charting the Day: Your Body Clocks

Just about everything you do is run by the clock—your own inner biological pacemaker known as the circadian clock, from the Latin *circa* ("about") and *diem* ("a day"). This timekeeper is hardwired into many cells throughout your body and runs on a twenty-four- to twenty-five-hour cycle that follows the turning of the globe.

The powerful master clock that keeps your time lies deep in your brain. Called the suprachiasmatic nucleus (SCN), this tiny but mighty clock paces all sorts of daily physiological fluctuations and cycles, including body temperature, blood pressure, heart rate, hormone levels, and sleep-waking times. It tells your brain's pineal gland when to release melatonin to promote sleep and when to shut it off to help you awaken.

Scientists have found that active clock genes are not just in the SCN, but are scattered throughout the body, so that some organs and tissues may be running on different schedules, with their mini-clocks responding to other external clues such as exercise, stress, and temperature changes.

Some of these clocks are accurate but inflexible, and others are less reliable but under your conscious control. They rule all of your functions and actions, and maybe even your life span, by determining the number of times your cells can divide.

The Best of Times?

Given all these ruling clocks, is there an absolute best time of day for differing activities? Perhaps. The field of chronobiology—the science of body time—is studying this now, with researchers in chronomedicine looking at the ways to match body cycles to medical care to maintain health and treat illnesses. Many body functions, diseases, and conditions peak and ebb at certain predictable times (see "A Time for Everything" on the following page). Every mom knows that childhood fevers rise at night, for example, and are lowest in the early morning, just as our temperatures when we are healthy follow that cycle. Doctors are finding that the timing of tests, treatments, or dosage may affect outcomes.

Your personal inner clock is unique, and understanding its rhythms may help you stay healthy longer. At the simplest level, people are either larks or owls: respectively, those who wake up and sleep early and those who perform best at late hours and prefer late rising. At its more sophisticated level, the time of day when patients receive chemotherapy, have surgery, or take daily medications or other treatments may have a great deal to do with their effectiveness. With the growing interest in patient-driven medicine and individualized medical care, circadian research is a fertile field.

A TIME FOR EVERYTHING: DAILY PATTERNS

Although each of us has a personal and slightly different body clock, surveys, observation, and research have found some overall patterns that follow the hours of the day. Your personal rhythm may not match the events listed here, of course, as the data are from many sources and represent an average.

1:00 A.M.	Pregnant women are most likely to go into labor.
	Immune cells called helper T lymphocytes are at their peak.
2:00 A.M.	Levels of growth hormone are highest.
4:00 A.M.	Body temperature and respiration at their lowest. Asthma attacks are most likely to occur.
6:00 A.M.	Onset of menstruation is most likely.
	Insulin levels in the bloodstream are lowest.
	Blood pressure and heart rate begin to rise beginning a four-hour time block when most heart attacks and strokes occur.
	Levels of the stress hormone cortisol increase.
	Levels of melatonin begin to fall, while levels of adenosine increase, to promote waking.
7:00 A.M.	Hay fever symptoms are worst.
7:30 A.M.	Secretion of melatonin stops.
8:00 A.M.	Highest risk for heart attack and stroke.
	Symptoms of rheumatoid arthritis are worst.
	Helper T lymphocytes are at their lowest daytime level.
	Bowel movement most likely.
10:00 A.M.	Beginning of highest alertness for early risers.
Noon	Level of hemoglobin in the blood is at its peak.
2:30 P.M.	Best coordination.
3:00 P.M.	Grip strength, respiratory rate, and reflex sensitivity are highest.
5:00 P.M.	Greatest cardiovascular and muscle strength.
6:00 P.M.	Urinary flow is highest.
6:30 P.M.	Blood pressure is highest.
7:00 P.M.	Body temperature is highest.
9:00 P.M.	Pain threshold is lowest.
	Melatonin secretion starts.
10:30 P.M.	Bowel movement suppressed.
11:00 P.M.	Allergic responses most likely.

Part 1

2
3
4

Coming to Consciousness

awake and aware

5 A.M. to 8 A.M.

5 *a.m.*

Waking to the World

One minute, you're dead to the world. In dreamland. Incommunicado. The next second, or so it seems, you and your brain are being dragged into the waking world.

The wakeup call can be the relentless shrilling of an alarm clock, a baby's cry, or the grind and beep of a garbage truck. Other senses—the smell and sound of brewing coffee, a shake or a splash of cold water, hunger, thirst, or an urge to urinate—can nudge you toward wakefulness. And with the first light, our body clocks chip in as well, setting off an ebb and flow of hormones and neurotransmitters to stimulate us to awareness.

The process of arousal actually takes several minutes and a literal brainstorm of neural activity with a complex combination of cues, neurochemicals, and body clocks to get you up and keep you awake.

Your Inner Alarm Clocks

A sentry system in your basic brain is set to arouse you when it detects change, such as that annoying alarm clock. Called the reticular activating system (RAS), it's a part of your brain left over from the prehistoric era when you had to be able to detect danger immediately and wake abruptly.

The RAS acts as a gatekeeper for incoming stimulation and sensations, perking up when it detects something new and helping your brain wake up and stay alert and awake all day long. It connects your brain-stem to your cortex, sensory organs, and limbic system to help process and regulate activity and consciousness in your thinking brain.

The RAS does this through fibers that project widely throughout your brain, many through the thalamus, considered to be the doorway between sensory input and the cerebral cortex. *Reticular* means "little net." Like a net, the fibers of the RAS "catch" signals from the sensory systems about what's happening in the body or its local environment.

A part of the RAS called the locus coeruleus is particularly attuned to respond to new, abrupt, or loud stimulation and is your brain's major factory for norepinephrine, a neurotransmitter released in response to stress or other stimulation. As soon as the system detects a significant change, such as a snarling sabre-toothed tiger, a splash of cold water, or that ringing alarm clock, it pops out some strong chemicals to increase your state of alertness.

Meanwhile, as night turns to day, another alarm clock starts to "ring." It's the built-in light-dark alarm system of your body clock called the suprachiasmatic nucleus (SCN): two tiny bundles of ten thousand neurons, each no bigger than a letter on this page, nestled deep in your brain, very near the optic nerves.

As the morning light strikes your retina, photoreceptor cells there signal to the neurons in the SCN to begin firing. The SCN toggles a biological switch setting off a process that tells the pineal gland to shut off the flow of melatonin, start the waking process, and keep you awake all day.

Your Brain Chemicals

While you were sleeping, levels of adenosine, a neurochemical with a powerful effect on your sleep-wake cycle, were dwindling. Your entire metabolism slowed, bottoming out to its lowest rate about an hour ago, at 4:00 A.M. or so. Now, as you come to consciousness, a brew of chemical messengers from your brain is telling your metabolism to get up and go.

The neurotransmitter acetylcholine helps pass information to the rest of your brain's sentry system for interpretation. As the amygdala detects a possible survival challenge (*There's an alarm!*), your hippo-campus helps decide how much focused attention and memory for-mation the stimulus warrants (it's a wake-up alarm, not a fire alarm) and helps it get processed by your thinking brain where goal setting and decisions are made (if you ignore that alarm and are late again, you can lose your job, so you better get up *now*).

Other neurotransmitters jump in, including serotonin (neces-sary for mood regulation and involuntary movement) and dopamine (needed for voluntary movement and attentiveness). A hefty shot of cortisol jump-starts everything. Your body temperature, blood pres-sure, and respiration begin to rise. And these arousal systems don't stop after they wake you. An active RAS is vital for ongoing aware-ness. In fact, if your brain's RAS stops firing signals, you may fall asleep again, and damage to your RAS can cause coma. Many general anes-thetics and some tranquilizers work on this part of your brain.

The SCN will also stay active most of the day, helping you stay awake until evening when the process reverses, and the rising levels of sleep-promoting chemicals such as melatonin and adenosine make you sleepy all over again.

Larks and Owls

The trip from sleep to consciousness seems longer for some people than others. Some of us seem to wake up instantly: as soon as our eyes pop open, we appear to be fully awake and often upright. Others strug-gle toward consciousness, moving and sometimes speaking but not fully connected for a half-hour or more, responding to a body clock set a bit later.

Some of us are morning people; some of us are not. Scientists don't know why yet, but all of us know which is which. In case you don't know which you are (or are not sure about someone else) here's a list of char-acteristics that makes it clear that larks and owls march to different body clocks.

The numbers in brackets are points you scored for each answer. You'll find out how to use them at the end of the questionnaire.

ARE YOU AN OWL OR A LARK?

1. Breakfast: How's your appetite in the first half-hour after you wake up in the morning?
   a. Very poor [1]
   b. Fairly poor [2]
   c. Fairly good [3]
   d. Very good [4]

2. For the first half-hour after you wake up in the morning, how do you feel?
   a. Very tired [1]
   b. Fairly tired [2]
   c. Fairly refreshed [3]
   d. Very refreshed [4]

3. When you have no commitments the next day, at what time do you go to bed compared to your usual bedtime?
   a. Seldom or never later [4]
   b. Less than one hour later [3]
   c. One to two hours later [2]
   d. More than two hours later [1]

4. You are starting a new fitness regime. A friend suggests joining his fitness class between 7:00 A.M. and 8:00 A.M. How do you think you'd perform?
   a. Would be in good form [4]
   b. Would be in reasonable form [3]
   c. Would find it difficult [2]
   d. Would find it very difficult [1]

5. At what time in the evening do you feel tired and in need of sleep?
   a. 8:00 P.M. to 9:00 P.M. [5]
   b. 9:00 P.M. to 10:15 P.M. [4]
   c. 1:15 A.M. to 1:45 A.M. [3]
   d. 1:45 A.M. to 2:00 A.M. [2]
   e. 2:00 A.M. to 3:00 A.M. [1]

continues on next page

6. If you went to bed at 11:00 P.M., how tired would you be?
   a. Not at all tired [0]
   b. A little tired [2]
   c. Fairly tired [3]
   d. Very tired [5]

7. One night you have to remain awake between 4:00 A.M. and 6:00 A.M. You have no commitments the next day. Which suits you best?
   a. Not to go to bed until 6:00 A.M. [1]
   b. Nap before 4:00 A.M. and sleep after 6:00 A.M. [2]
   c. Sleep before 4:00 A.M. and nap after 6:00 A.M. [3]
   d. Sleep before 4 A.M. and remain awake after 6:00 A.M. [4]

8. Suppose that you can choose your own work hours but have to work five hours in the day. When would you like to start your workday?
   a. Midnight to 5:00 A.M. [1]
   b. 3:00 A.M. to 8:00 A.M. [5]
   c. 8:00 A.M. to 10:00 A.M. [4]
   d. 10:00 A.M. to 2:00 P.M. [3]
   e. 2:00 P.M. to 4:00 P.M. [2]
   f. 4:00 P.M. to midnight [1]

9. At what time of day do you feel your best?
   a. Midnight to 5:00 A.M. [1]
   b. 5:00 A.M. to 9:00 A.M. [5]
   c. 9:00 A.M. to 11:00 A.M. [4]
   d. 11:00 A.M. to 1:00 P.M. [3]
   e. 5:00 P.M. to 10:00 P.M. [2]
   f. 10:00 P.M. to midnight [1]

10. Do you think of yourself as a morning or evening person?
    a. Morning type [6]
    b. More morning than evening [4]
    c. More evening than morning [2]
    d. Evening type [0]

Scoring: Add up the points you scored for each answer. The maximum score for these questions is 46. The minimum is 8. The higher your score, the more of a morning person you are. The lower the score, the more you're a night owl.

Coming to Our Senses

As you swing out of bed and start your morning ritual, your senses wake up to guide you through the day. Taking your morning shower, brushing your teeth, tying your shoes: you probably don't give any of

---

WHY DO MEN AWAKE WITH ERECTIONS?

Waking up with an erection is fairly common for a healthy male. In fact, an erect penis may be the default state. (Women also have nighttime erections. But more about that later. See "10:00 P.M.")

Nocturnal erections don't (usually) have much to do with sexy dreams or the need to urinate. Men have three to five cycles of nocturnal penile tumescence through the night during phrases of rapid eye movement (REM) sleep. Women go through the same cycle, with an engorgement of the labia, vagina, and clitoris.

These erections don't usually wake us up, and researchers still don't know exactly why they happen. Some speculate this ebb and flow over the long hours of sleep is part of nature's way of keeping a blood supply to the sex organs.

Others think an erect organ may be the default state. Most of the time, the sympathetic nervous system puts the brakes on many functions, including erections, and it's known that the sympathetic neurons in the locus coeruleus that connect to the spinal cord are turned off during REM sleep. This may allow nocturnal erections to occur.

Researchers are interested in morning erections as a clue to solving erection problems. If a man who has erectile dysfunction is getting morning erections, the cause could be psychological rather than physical. There hasn't been much interest among researchers in women's nocturnal turn-ons.

this much thought, and you don't need to. Your brain is directing these actions on a subconscious level. (See "Your Brain Prefers Autopilot," page 24.)

But no matter how simple (or unconscious) the action, each involves a multiplicity of complex memory, sensory, and muscle functions that, not surprisingly, involve many regions of the brain and frequently overlap with incoming data from other senses.

Take the simple act of getting a cup of coffee. You smell the coffee: it triggers a memory that you like and want coffee. You look around and see the coffee pot, hear it perking and bubbling, and get up and walk across the room and pour a cup. In just the milliseconds that your frontal lobes decide to get that cup of coffee, a tidal wave of neural signals sweeps across a multitude of brain regions.

An Orchestra of Sensory Harmony

Each step in the act of getting your coffee draws on a different combination of senses and brain regions to receive and interpret these incoming data. Your brain has to coordinate vision and sound with balance, touch, smell, and spatial awareness. It has to decide which muscles to activate to move you across the room and how much pressure to use when you pick up the cup and coffee pot, when to tip the pot and when to stop pouring coffee, whether the brew tastes strong enough for you, if it needs sugar or milk, if it's too hot or too cool.

Smell pulled you toward the brew. It's our most intense and ancient sense, profoundly connected to memory, sex, and survival. Even bacteria "smell" poisons or nutrients, danger or safety. Smell helps us select our sex mates and remember the good and bad. Many animals rely on smell to know the sex, social rank, territories, and reproductive status of others and to identity their own mates or offspring.

Smell is profoundly linked with memory. Just think how suddenly a familiar scent can whisk you into the past, even many decades ago. Proust surely did: he wrote thirty-two hundred pages featuring the power of memory, spurred by the remembered taste and smell of a small French cake, the madeleine.

Research shows he was right: smell can help the brain encode memories. Volunteers in one study memorized the locations of several objects while smelling a rose scent; then some of them were exposed to the same scent while they slept. Those with perfumed sleep remembered the locations of the objects much better than their fragrance-free peers did, because the scent probably reactivated memories stored temporarily in the hippocampus.

And no wonder. While human sense of smell is relatively weak compared to that of other mammals, we nevertheless have 347 different types of sensory neurons in the olfactory layer for smell inside the nose. Each one detects a different type of odor, and all the varied aromas and stenches we know result from mixtures of responses of these 347 types of receptor cells. By comparison with sight, for example,

---

THE VERY SMELL OF COFFEE MAY HELP THE RAT RACE

As you inhale that coffee aroma, the very smell intensifies alertness, partly because our brain remembers it as the scent of waking.

There may be a scientific basis for that coffee high. It seems that the aroma of coffee alone could be helpful to the stressed-out brain—in rats, at least, according to a report in the *Journal of Agricultural and Food Chemistry.*

Scientists had laboratory rats, including some that were sleep deprived, inhale the aroma of roasted coffee beans. They found the smell activated seventeen different genes in their brains, and thirteen of them produced proteins known to protect nerve cells from the damaging effects of stress. The experiment hasn't been tried on humans yet (the rat brains were dissected for the study), but it's known that caffeine also offsets the effects of adenosine, a sleep-promoting hormone.

You can conduct your own nonscientific study without shelling out four dollars for that latte. Just walk by the counter instead, inhaling deeply. The smell alone might be enough to kick-start your day.

every color we see results from signal combinations of only three types of sensory neurons in the retina (red-, green-, or blue-sensitive cones).

Vision shows you where to go as information streams in through your retina, moving through the optic nerve to the thalamus and then to the occipital cortex. There your brain has to make various adjustments to "see" the coffee pot. Since light was criss-crossed when it passed through the lens, it was received upside down. And since the optic nerves partially cross over at the optic chasm, each hemisphere of the brain receives slightly different input from both eyes. Your brain combines the data for a three-dimensional effect and then neatly turns the image right-side-up. Finally, the parietal and temporal lobes interpret what the brain is "seeing."

Sound helps you orient yourself in time and space. It enters the eardrums and travels through several complex processing and filtering centers, including the thalamus, and ends up in the temporal gyrus of our thinking brain where it is interpreted and processed further. Speech, for example, gets shunted to the left hemisphere language centers.

Touch and Movement: Feeling Our Way

If smell is our most ancient sense, touch is our first sense as a newborn. It floods our brain with sensation as we waken and is vital for movement, guiding us as we get up and head for the kitchen. Touch signals are processed in a brain area directly behind the fold called the central sulcus, an area associated with movement. (For more about movement see "7:00 P.M.") Touch tells us when our fingers encounter the coffee cup and have grasped it, and it guides the move toward our lips.

Scientists are still trying to figure out how touch works on a molecular level, because the nerve endings in question are extremely small and there are so very many of them. Our entire bodies are covered with a network of tactile sensors, perhaps 6 million to 10 million in all. Interpreting touch sensation can be tricky, since there's not a lot of detailed information about exactly where these information gatherers are located.

Sensory receptors are not evenly distributed over your body. We have many fewer touch sensors in our internal organs, and the surface of the brain feels nothing at all when touched. But the skin (our largest organ), especially the erogenous zones and the area around the mouth, is rich in receptors. Your lips are hundreds of times more sensitive than, say, the rough soles of your feet.

But you already knew that. In fact, we all know, through painful experience, which areas of our body have the most sensory receptors and receivers.

Varieties of Touch

Touch has the potential for adding pleasure and pain to your world and is essential for protecting your body from damage. Those who cannot feel, including pain, can't retreat from damage. This is why some people with leprosy or diabetes who have lost the nerves for pain perception often end up with extremities so damaged they must be amputated.

The signals and feelings that arise from your body surface—itch, sharp pain, dull pain, burning pain, tickle, soothing touch, heat and cold—go to the insula and anterior cingulate cortex. Sensations from the inside of your body—the invigorating inner feeling when you finally drink that first cup of warm morning coffee—are mapped in your insula.

Researchers make a distinction between passive and active touch information. Passive tactile awareness is accepting external sensations: the sun on your face, the wind in your hair, the warmth of a morning shower, your mother's caress. Active touching is when we explore our surroundings with our hands, feet, or mouth: sipping that coffee, walking barefoot on wet grass, biting into a ripe mango. This form of touch helps our brains develop a comprehensive understanding of objects around us.

Both active and passive touch are vital for early brain development. Babies of many species develop as they actively explore their environment with hands, feet, and mouth.

YOUR BRAIN PREFERS AUTOPILOT: IT SAVES FUEL

As you get up and go about these morning rituals, you probably don't give them much thought—and you don't need to. The many regions of your brain directing these actions operate on a subconscious level. And that's just the way your brain likes it.

Tasks that require practice—like brushing and flossing your teeth properly, playing the piano, or riding a bike—must be learned consciously. Your brain has to concentrate. But once you've mastered them, your brain shuffles them to a lower level of consciousness: you don't "think" about what you're doing. In fact, if you focus too much attention on the details, you can bungle the performance.

Your brain likes this auto-state and is constantly trying to run on autopilot. It wants to remove mental processes from consciousness, so that work can be completed faster, more effectively, and at a lower metabolic cost.

That's because consciousness is slow, subject to error, and expensive. It involves chemical reactions and changes in synaptic connections that take lots of oxygen and glucose. In other words, it takes more energy. But with practice and mastery, the neural networks involved gradually become smaller and get shifted to areas that operate unconsciously, such as the motor cortex, the cerebellum, and the basal ganglia.

Passive touch is vital as well, and therapeutic massage is part of regular health care in many cultures. Many researchers agree that early skin-to-skin contact affects later intelligence, as well as social and emotional growth. In the laboratory, young rats separated from their mother immediately secrete less growth hormone.

Human babies left untouched for too long, as many children have been in orphanages, don't develop normally in many ways. Studies show, for example, that children who spent the first two years of their lives in an orphanage may later produce much lower levels of oxytocin, the hormone of bonding, love, and trust. In fact, therapies for premature babies that include whole-body massage have been shown to reduce stress hormone levels and are correlated with faster weight gain and growth.

6 *a.m.*

Coming to Consciousness

By 6:00 A.M., your brain has your mind up and about—more or less. But "who" is waking up? And what is "consciousness"? Waking up often feels as if we've been away and the mind is returning to the body. If so, where was it?

Consciousness is one of the great unsolved puzzles of neuroscience. We know it when we experience it. But what is it? And where does it live in the brain? The problem is so challenging that for a long time, it was left to philosophers. But with newer imaging techniques, researchers are gradually identifying the pieces of the puzzle.

And there are many. While philosophers may refer to *the* consciousness, scientists say consciousness is actually many states or levels along a continuum. At one end of the spectrum is alertness or vigilance: the one that science (and we) define as being awake and aware. At the other end is deep sleep and coma.

Neural networks lace through your entire brain. But so far researchers believe that we can consciously access only some brain activities that happen within the cortex. Special imaging techniques suggest that we consciously perceive only the information that gets processed in what's called the associative regions of the cerebral cortex—the four lobes of the thinking brain.

The Seat of Consciousness

The associative regions of the cerebral cortex help with the conscious perception and identity of your own body: the planning of movement, spatial perception and awareness, orientation, and imagination. The associative cortex is strongly connected to the amygdala in the limbic system (our center for emotional memory) and the hippocampus (our organizer of cognitive memory).

When you awaken, the prefrontal cortex goes to work as soon as you start thinking about what you will do today. It's the foundation of the thinking brain, making conscious plans, solving problems, and processing thoughts. It cooperates with the orbitofrontal cortex, which is occupied with goals as well as with the consequences of your actions. Some researchers say this is the seat of morals, ethics, and—possibly–conscience.

The temporal lobe of the associative cortex, which borders the occipital lobe, helps you recognize scenes, objects, and faces like your bedroom, your alarm clock, and the face on the pillow next to you. It

---

BIG-BRAINED BAMBOOZLERS

Our species, *Homo sapiens,* has big brains. So do our relatives, the monkeys and apes. Typically, brain size among species rises with increasing body size and metabolic demand. According to that formula, humans, monkeys, and apes have the brain volume of creatures twice as large as they are. Most of the enlargement comes from massive development of the neocortex (cerebral cortex).

In an interesting correlation of brain size and actions, a 2004 study shows that the use of deception by primate species rises along with increases in the volume of the brain's neocortex. That is, the members of species with the beefiest brains are most inclined to deceive one another (and perhaps any creature that might be an enemy or predator). Human brain size, of course, outranks all other animals on the body size chart.

also processes sounds, melodies, and language, like the morning news on your clock radio. The language center known as Wernicke's area is found here (in the brain's left hemisphere in most people). It registers the meaning of words and simple sentences, such as, "Aren't you out of the shower *yet*?"

Emotion, Memory, and Consciousness

You'll never forget some days and how you felt: the joy of the birth of your first child, the horror of the 9/11 terrorist attack, the pain of a near-death car accident. Your emotions make the events and your experience of them ever vivid; your memory keeps them alive.

Consciousness, memory, and emotion are inextricably intertwined. Here's what research is showing about how they connect in your brain.

The amygdala, the mighty nucleus of the limbic system (your emotional brain), has a major role here. Emotions are shaped below the level of your conscious thought ("subcortically," as neurobiologists say) by both memories and by the workings of your limbic system on the thinking brain (cerebral cortex).

The amygdala generates and processes unconscious emotional states and experiences. Its main job is to recognize input from your environment that is considered terrifying or could be physically damaging and signal you to fight or flee. Some researchers believe that the amygdala also takes part in non-fear-related emotions, such as curiosity and the will to action.

The emotions of desire, satisfaction, and contentment are closely related to the nucleus accumbens and the ventral tegmental area: your brain's so-called reward circuit. These act with the neurotransmitter dopamine and other powerful brain chemicals to alert the cerebral cortex and other brain centers when they detect a positive or desirable circumstance.

Memory content is critical to consciousness and to determining which experiences are dangerous or desirable. Brain researchers call conscious memory "declarative memory." Scientists differentiate between two types of declarative memory. Semantic memory is about information not related directly to people, locations, or time: it's generalized or factual information without (necessarily) specific context, such as the multiplication tables. Episodic memory is about experiences relating to the self. The very heart of episodic memory is the autobiographical memory, which forms the foundation of the self and self-awareness. According to current theory, the hippocampus is responsible for episodic memory, and the surrounding cortex controls semantic memory.

Between the limbic system (emotions) and the cerebral cortex (thought) sits the cingulate cortex. It's involved in controlling alertness and the emotional coloring of our internal reactions to physical sensations such as pain. In addition, the cingulate cortex works closely with the frontal lobe to control the recognition and correction of mistakes, a process vital to memory and survival.

It's Always About Networking

There's no consensus about how consciousness works. Some researchers believe it's a collective effort among many neurons, but they don't quite understand how clusters of neurons from the various regions of the brain get together and collaborate to form consciousness. Others say that specific conscious perceptions correspond to specific groups of neurons or parts of the brain, or that consciousness is a process rather than a place in the brain.

They do agree that the development of consciousness seems to rely on the huge number of links among neurons within the cortex. There are many more internal connections than there are points for exit and entry, which could mean that your thinking brain "talks" more to itself than with the parts of your brain that control sensory input and movement.

Some states of consciousness are thought to be based on split-second rewiring in the neural networks of the cortex to do a specific task. The connections in the synapses between the billions of neurons in the cortex can be strengthened or weakened for a short time to let nerve cells from specific sections of the networks temporarily share information—a short-term team effort, kind of like a community coming together for a barn raising.

Little Gray Cells and Big White Matter: Myelin in Your Brain

So far it seems that consciousness is most likely confined to what Agatha Christie's fictional detective Hercule Poirot famously called our "little gray cells": the neurons in the thinking parts of your brain. But it turns out your brain's big white matter plays a major role in making those gray cells work properly.

The gray cells make up the densely packed gray matter in the cortex: it's the "topsoil" of your brain that does your thinking, calculating, and decision making, says R. Douglas Fields, an expert in nervous system development. But underneath this thin layer is the brain's bedrock of white matter, filling up nearly half of the human brain—a far larger percentage than found in the brains of other animals.

For a long time, scientists thought this white matter was mostly passive and acted only as insulation for the long arms (axons) of your nerves. They now think the functioning of white matter may be just as critical as gray matter to how people master mental and social skills and may explain why it's hard for old dogs to learn new tricks.

White matter in your brain is made up of the millions of communications cables that string among your neurons, each cable containing a long, individual "wire" (an axon) coated with a white, fatty substance called myelin. That coating is crucial to cellular communication, in particular to how speedily and efficiently impulses race along the pathways in the thinking, sensory, and motor processing regions of your brain.

Studies are showing that the amount of white matter correlates directly with IQ: the more white matter, the higher the IQ. New studies also show that the extent of white matter varies in people who have different mental experiences: children who have been severely neglected have up to 17 percent less myelin in the corpus callosum, the connector between the brain's two hemispheres.

Myelin is only partially formed at birth and gradually develops in different brain regions through our twenties, working its way up from the hindbrain to the forebrain.

"White matter is key to types of learning that require prolonged practice and repetition, as well as extensive integration among greatly separated regions of the cerebral cortex," says Fields. "Children whose brains are still myelinating widely find it much easier to acquire new skills than their grandparents do."

This may explain why there seem to be windows for learning. Brain imaging of people of differing ages playing musical instruments shows that those who begin in childhood early in the myelination process had myelin distributed throughout the brain. But the brains of those who took up the same instrument as adults show increased white matter only in the forebrain—the part of the brain still undergoing myelination. It may also partly explain how the timing of myelination and the degree of completion can affect self-control (and why teenagers may lack it) and some mental illnesses. There is less white matter in the brains of people with schizophrenia, attention-deficit/hyperactivity disorder (ADHD), bipolar disease, autism, and even those who are pathological liars.

Faulty or missing myelin is responsible for a number of diseases, including multiple sclerosis and cerebral palsy. There's evidence that problems with myelination contribute to other conditions too. Dyslexia, for example, results from disrupted timing of communication in circuits for reading; brain imaging has revealed reduced white matter in these tracts, which could cause such disruption. The white matter abnormalities are thought to reflect both defects in the myelination process and abnormalities in the development of neurons affecting these white matter connections.

Here's the other bad news: myelin is regularly being broken down and restored in the brain, but after middle age—say forty-five or so—the replacement process begins to slow. We all have some gradual loss of myelin as we age, which is one of the reasons athletes lose their edge, our reflexes slow when confronted with a car running a red light, and we find it harder to learn to play tennis or chess.

One disheartening study of motor reflex reaction time and myelin suggests that reflex speed peaks at age thirty-nine and that it's related to myelin loss. Moreover, other brain functions, including memory, are

WHY DOES THE OUTER SURFACE OF THE BRAIN HAVE FOLDS?

In the nineteenth century, some scientists thought that the brain's surface shape was related to its function. As brain science progressed, these ideas seemed naive. But modern techniques are showing that these scientists were at least partly right: the landscape of the brain correlates with some brain function after all.

It's known that thought and all other forms of conscious experience happen in the cerebral cortex, the outermost layer of the brain, and that's why it's so convoluted. Over the course of evolution as human brains got bigger, we needed more space to house that brain than the skull had available. Folds allow more brain surface area without increasing the size of the head. In fact, the tissue sheet of your cerebral cortex is about three times as large as the inside surface of the skull.

This folding pattern is far from random. Nerve fiber bundles are tense, like stretched elastic. Regions in the brain that are densely connected are pulled toward one another, producing outward bulges between them—the hills of the cortical landscape. Weakly connected regions drift apart, forming cortical valleys. The stretching and compression of brain tissue also have an effect on the architecture of the cortex and the shape of individual cells.

affected. Myelin loss is possibly connected with age-related diseases such as Alzheimer's disease.

As Fields notes, you can still learn new skills after midlife, but you won't become a world-class piano, chess, or tennis competitor—at least based on what we know now.

Prime Time for Heart Attack and Stroke

Morning waking can be risky business. Surveys show the peak times for stroke and heart attacks are between 6:00 A.M. and noon. No one really knows why, but it could be because the neurotransmitters and hormones related to waking and stress—adrenaline, vasopressin, cortisol—are doing their jobs. It may also be related to the stress some of us feel when we wake on a workday and contemplate the situations awaiting us.

This is the period of the sharpest blood pressure rise. Cortisol floods your system with levels ten to twenty times as high as when you are sleeping. It jump-starts your body to get you into action quickly, raising body temperature and speeding up your heart, with blood pressure peaking shortly after you awake.

The chemical rush can be hard on your brain and your heart, especially if your blood vessels are less elastic, you have high blood pressure, or you have plaque buildup in your arteries, The sudden jump may stress already vulnerable hearts or shake clots loose. Once you're up, cortisol ebbs back, and the blood vessel constrictor noradrenaline takes over to maintain alertness.

7 a.m.

Those Morning Emotions

So angry so early?

Alas, the first appearance of anger, conflict, and just plain crankiness hits our brains early in the day. It's a harried time when most of us are not at our best. It's especially fraught for live-togethers who are trying to get out the door: parents, partners, kids, even roomies.

The trigger could be about who's taking the kids to school, who used the last drop of milk, even whose turn it is to do the dishes, and it could quickly ramp up to where you feel as if you could do serious harm. Your blood pressure goes up, way up, and you slam doors, break dishes, or storm out of the house to prevent more violence.

Whew. Your emotional brain is in the driver's seat, and your reason is being taken for a ride.

Certainly there are reasons to be irritable, and your brain is ready to react to them—or at least, your amygdala is. Anger has its roots in the old amygdala, the almond-sized emotional center of the brain that is the seat of vigilance and basic emotions such as fear and aggression.

As the morning's array of sensory impressions flows into the thalamus, the brain's major sensory reception and sorting area, the trigger-happy amygdala is poised to react. At a perceived threat, such as a nasty quip in the kitchen, it can flip the switch that prompts the hypothalamus to set off a neurochemical chain reaction. It recruits stress chemicals such as cortisol and noradrenalin from the adrenal gland to put your body on high alert and increase stress, frustration, and, yes, anger.

There are brakes for all those raw emotions. Serotonin (the versatile neurotransmitter of emotional balance and good moods) and the ventral area of the prefrontal cortex (known to be crucial for constraining impulsive outbursts) damp down reactions such as anger.

But sometimes the prefrontal cortex is just not up to the job, especially first thing in the morning. It gets overwhelmed by the amygdala, and no wonder: there are many more neural connections going from the amygdala to the cerebral cortex than the other way. And studies suggest that aggressive people tend to have a less active prefrontal lobe in general.

Reason Needs a Neurochemical Boost

Skipping breakfast might contribute to that anger in the early morning. As your mom used to say when you got cranky, "Eat something already." She may have called it low blood sugar. Science is saying it's more likely low serotonin.

Serotonin is made from the amino acid tryptophan, which can be obtained only through what we eat. So when we haven't eaten for awhile, as in the early morning, our serotonin levels go down and our tendency toward irritation can go up.

Scientists have long known that serotonin is involved in emotion. It's the key neurotransmitter affected by the class of antidepressants such as Prozac called selective serotonin reuptake inhibitors (SSRIs). These work by increasing the levels of serotonin in your brain and helping keep your emotions on an even keel.

Multiple studies connect low brain serotonin in men—and in criminals—with impulsive and often violent acts. This connection may also involve testosterone, since studies don't show the same connection between violence and low serotonin in women.

Serotonin's role in emotional control is still uncertain, but it appears to be connected to aggression and anger and the brain's ability to control anger. It seems that when serotonin levels are low, we are less likely to be able to control our responses when our hot button gets pushed. Low serotonin levels are associated with obsessive compulsive disorder, anxiety, depression, and a multitude of other feeling-not-so-good conditions.

It's also involved in our perceptions of what's fair, and that combination can get the day off to a rollicking start. In one study, scientists temporarily lowered serotonin levels in a group of people and had them play a money game based on fair and unfair offers to split the loot. Others with normal serotonin levels also played. Those with lowered serotonin perceived unfairness in low offers more often, and when they lost, they retaliated by depriving other players of money as well. The study showed a direct link between serotonin levels and aggressive behavior, according to study author Molly Crockett, a psychologist at the University of Cambridge, and colleagues.

Since serotonin depends on tryptophan, it's made up from what you eat. Among the best sources are foods rich in protein and hot

---

SOOTHING THE CRANKY MORNING BEAST

It's hard to put on the brakes once your brain is rocketing down the road to rage, but you may be able to prevent provoking your amygdala by changing some things in your schedule:

- Plan ahead to limit decisions and conflicts. Lay out clothes, and get lunches, papers, bus passes, and toll booth change ready the night before.

- Avoid a time crunch by setting the alarm to get up a bit earlier.

- Eat breakfast to boost serotonin.

- Add a few minutes of stretching, tai chi, or yoga; some deep breathing; or ten minutes of prayer or meditation. All are shown to lower the anger response, and meditation might avert some of that morning stress.

chocolate, oats, bananas, milk, yogurt, and eggs. Hmm. Sounds like breakfast to us.

Can Meditation Help Master Those Emotions?

Millions of us begin the day with early morning prayer or meditation and find it does our brain good. It can go right to our head, quieting usually vigilant centers and sharpening our thinking centers to leave us feeling centered with a calmness and clarity that lasts well into the day.

No wonder. Imaging studies are showing that long-term meditation practice can change brain structure, thickening the cortex, changing the type and rhythm of brain waves, and honing the ability to focus. It can also lower anxiety, blood pressure, and stress.

Meditation is an ancient practice to quiet and focus the mind on an object, idea, or sensation or on simply being still in the moment. The aim is to not be caught up in thoughts and emotions as they swirl by.

Meditation practice can help your brain learn how to diffuse anger and other negative emotions, research shows. Richard Davidson of the University of Wisconsin–Madison, himself a meditator, has been looking into the brains of Tibetan monks and other long-time meditators to see what's going on when they sit in meditation. The Dalai Lama, the spiritual leader of Tibet, has encouraged such research, convincing reclusive Tibetan monks with decades of meditating experience to have their brains imaged.

Tibetan Buddhist monks spend a great portion of every day meditating. An important goal is to detach themselves from feelings, especially negative feelings, and to cultivate loving kindness toward all living creatures. These lifelong meditators have said that they experience much less anxiety, grief, or annoyance than nonmeditators, although many of them have faced physical and emotional challenges during the decades of conflict with China.

When Davidson's colleagues imaged the brains of eight meditating monks, they found the monks had significantly higher levels of so-called gamma waves, which have frequencies ranging from 25 to 42 hertz and appear during periods of increased awareness. They are produced by active neurons in the neocortex and associated with consciousness and perception. The gamma wave levels of the meditating monks were two or three times the resting level, greater than any ever before reported in scientific literature except in pathological cases. This effect was especially pronounced in two regions of the frontal lobes involved in modulating emotions. Eight volunteers who had just been taught how to meditate and who acted as controls showed little gamma wave gain. Davidson sees this as neuronal evidence of the monks' ability to master their feelings.

In a different study that did not involve meditators, researchers looked at brain activity as people were shown disturbing images. They noted that those who used strategies to mentally distance themselves coped better and had more activity in the prefrontal cortex. When the frontal lobe neurons were more active, the neurons of the limbic (or emotional) system were quieter, especially in the amygdala.

Is There a God Spot in Your Brain?

Meditation is not usually considered a religious practice, but it resembles some prayer practices, such as saying the rosary, chanting, and concentrating on the concept of oneness with God. And while the mind at prayer has not been studied as much as the meditating mind, some studies of the brains of praying nuns have shown activity similar to that of meditating monks.

But where does that spiritual urge come from? Are our brains hardwired for spirituality? Because spiritual quests and mystical experiences are as old as time and exist in every culture, scientists are wondering if there is a specific place in the brain that creates or responds to a concept of God. There are even names for this new field of study: *neurotheology* and *spiritual neuroscience.*

Using the tools of modern neuroscience, researchers are trying to discover what's going on in the brain when people have spiritual experiences during prayer and meditation. Some scientists think these experiences happen in a specific section of the brain—the temporal lobe—but studies convince others that the biological basis of spirituality is much broader.

So far they haven't pinned it down in spite of imaging techniques that allow researchers to look into the brains of people as they pray, meditate, or experience mystical highs. They are finding activity in the brain at these times, but it's not in the same place or at the same strength for everyone or for every practice.

No two mystics describe their experiences in the same way, and it's difficult to distinguish among the various types of mystical experiences. They can be spiritual, traditionally religious, or, to add to the ambiguity, reflect awe of the universe or of nature.

The brains of Buddhist meditators were imaged as they reported reaching a state in which they lose a sense of individual separateness. At that point, images showed a big drop of activity in the parietal lobe (which coordinates incoming sensory data) and an increase in activity in the right prefrontal cortex (an area involved in planning and attentiveness). A study that scanned the brains of several hundred meditating Buddhists found something similar, but the activity was in the left prefrontal cortex. Moreover, the most experienced meditators had the least amount of brain activity.

Brain imaging of praying Franciscan nuns found similar brain activity, but a study of those "speaking in tongues" showed a drop in prefrontal lobe activity. And a small study of nuns remembering experiences of communicating with God showed activity in the insula, a spot connected with social emotions, and in the caudate nucleus, an area involved with, among other things, falling in love.

The diversity of brain regions involved in the nuns' religious experience shows the complexity of spirituality. "There is no single God spot, localized uniquely in the temporal lobe of the human brain," says Mario Beauregard, who conducted studies with nuns. "These states are mediated by a neural network that is well distributed throughout the brain."

Researchers are finding that spiritual practices can have positive effects. Recent findings suggest that meditation can improve the ability to pay attention. Davidson and his colleagues at the University of Wisconsin–Madison asked seventeen people who had received three months of intensive training in meditation and twenty-three meditation novices to perform an attention task in which they had to successively pick out two numbers embedded in a series of letters. The novices did what most other people do: they missed the second number because they were still focusing on the first—a phenomenon called attentional blink. In contrast, all the trained meditators consistently picked out both numbers, indicating that practicing meditation can improve focus.

Meditation may even delay certain signs of aging in the brain, according to preliminary work by neuroscientist Sara Lazar of Harvard University and her colleagues. A 2005 paper in *NeuroReport* noted that twenty experienced meditators showed greater thickness in certain brain regions compared to fifteen people who did not meditate. In particular, the prefrontal cortex and right anterior insula were between four- and eight-thousandths of an inch thicker in the meditators; the oldest of the meditators boasted the greatest increase in thickness, the reverse of the usual process of aging.

It could be that different kinds of spiritual feelings come from different parts of the brain. Or, some say, such spiritual feelings may be no more than a blip in the brain's electrical circuit or even an epileptic event. Those with temporal lobe epilepsy tend to have more spiritual episodes, and mild electromagnetic stimulation there produced religious bliss in some but not all.

Whatever the source or wherever it happens, praying and meditation can leave us happier and, some say, healthier, leading researchers to search for other ways we could send anyone's brain to the same place.

Practice Makes Compassion

Prayer and meditation may also help your brain learn compassion. A study of long-term meditators found that concentrating on feelings of loving kindness physically affects brain regions that play a role in empathy and suggests people can be trained to cultivate this positive emotion.

Antoine Lutz and his colleagues, including Davidson, took functional magnetic resonance imaging (fMRI) scans of the brains of sixteen veteran meditators (some of them Tibetan monks) as well as sixteen others who were beginners. They measured blood flow in the brains of both when they were not meditating and as they meditated on compassionate feelings while hearing a woman's screams or a baby laughing.

When the expert meditators were focused on compassionate meditation and heard the sound of a woman in distress, the insula burst into action. And when these expert meditators heard the female screams or the sound of a baby laughing, their brains showed more activity than those of the novices in areas like the right temporal parietal juncture, which plays a role in understanding another's emotion.

The research doesn't prove that compassion can be learned, but it opens the possibility, and that could have implications for treating a range of disorders, including depression. This compassion might also make it easier to avoid conflict at home and abroad.

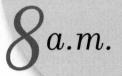

8 a.m.

Finding Your Way

As you leave home in the morning, you probably don't think about how to get where you're going when you've gone there before. That's partly your brain's memory for landmarks. Your hippocampus, a pair of tiny seahorse-shaped structures deep in the brain, is known to help create new memories, mark our movements through space, and help place our life events in a time line. But it may also be due to a process that involves specialized neurons that mark where you've been on a mental map.

Researchers postulate that we create mental maps of our environments. They've discovered cells in the hippocampus that fire when we are in specific locations (they are called place cells) and that these help us organize our experiences and the places where they happened on "cognitive maps."

Working with rats, they've also discovered grid cells, which are even more specialized than place cells, in a nearby part of the brain called the entorhinal cortex. When they studied the brain actions in rats let loose in a large area, they found the rat brains have specialized neurons that project a latticework of triangles across the mental map of an environment, and that cells fire as the rats moved to specific spots on the grid, tracking their path and location.

It's an astounding discovery that is still under study. So far, only grid cells in rat brains have been studied. But it is known that most mammals share systems of navigation. And this understanding suggests how we can constantly update information about our position on that internal cognitive map and relate it to personal memories about our experiences in time and space. Some researchers also believe the spatial data in the grid cells help the hippocampus create the context needed to form and store autobiographical memories.

Meanwhile, just plain memory for landmarks goes a long way to explain how we find our way—that and reading actual maps, and here we find that the brains of some male and female mammals have different systems.

Why His Brain May Not Ask for Directions

Finding your way to a new place by estimating distances and orientation is referred to as *dead reckoning,* and men do better at it than women. Women, on the other brain, may do better at navigating by remembering landmarks and reading directions.

In men, parts of the parietal cortex, which is involved in spatial perception, are relatively bigger than the same brain regions in women. In women, however, brain imaging shows that the hippocampus, which is involved in memory storage as well as spatial perception and mapping of the environment, is larger than in men.

These differences might explain why and how men and women use different techniques in finding their way—but not why men refuse to ask directions even when they are hopelessly lost. Could it be that directions based on landmarks don't help a brain dead-set on dead reckoning?

Experiments with rats show much the same pattern: male rats are more likely to navigate mazes using directional and positional information, while female rats are more likely to navigate the same mazes using available landmarks, says neuroscientist Larry Cahill, who is researching learning and memory.

Investigators have yet to demonstrate, however, that male rats are less likely than females to ask for directions, Cahill notes.

BEEN THERE, DONE THAT:
COULD DÉJÀ VU BE EXPLAINED BY GRID CELLS?

"This is a great question, because grid cells, which are involved in processing spatial information about our surroundings, are located in a brain region that is part of a larger memory system thought to be responsible for the feeling of familiarity," says neuroscientist Edvard I. Moser of the Norwegian University of Science and Technology. However, Moser (whose team discovered grid cells) thinks it more likely that place cells play a stronger role in our sense that a new locale is familiar—a feeling called "déjà visité."

Your brain is working to keep track of distinct locations within your surrounding area (say, at the kitchen table versus in front of the refrigerator). Place cells correspond to a specific location in an environment and fire when you pass through that spot. These cells are in the hippocampus.

Your brain also notes how these different locales relate to one another (the table is three feet to the right of the fridge, for instance). Grid cells work in a network and become active across several regularly spaced points in any setting. Grid cells are located in the entorhinal cortex, a brain region that processes information before sending it to the hippocampus. The geometrical arrangement of these cells, relative to one another and to the external setting, ultimately helps us form a mental map of a certain environment.

Because we know that place cells have a unique firing pattern for nearly every experience, it's likely that the hippocampus, and not primarily the entorhinal cortex, decides whether a location is new or being revisited.

To simplify all of this, when you're in a new place and feel as if you've been down this road (or in this place) before, it may be the place cells at that new location are similar to those from a place or time in the past.

How We Know Where to Find Our Lost Keys

Having trouble finding your keys—again? Your better half, or maybe your kids, rag you mercilessly about it: you're always losing and finding those keys, even when they are in plain sight.

You may forget where you put something, but it seems your brain has a system for remembering and visually locating specific objects. Researchers call it feature-based attention—essentially the tuning of your visual processing system to specific colors, shapes, or motions as a way of formulating an awareness of a scene—in other words, picking up on patterns. This is the mechanism that allows you to find things when you know *what* they are but you don't know *where* they are.

Researchers set out to see how this happens. John Serences, a cognitive scientist at the University of California, Irvine, and Geoffrey Boynton, a system neurobiologist at the Salk Institute for Biological Studies in La Jolla, California, had ten people perform a visual attention task while their brains were being scanned by functional magnetic resonance imaging (fMRI). During the test, participants faced a screen in which the bottom half was empty, while the top half showed clusters of dots that moved.

Neuroscientists know from previous work on spatial attention that varying groups of neurons in the visual cortex process different sections of the visual field. A subset of neurons will fire—that is, send electrical signals that convey information—when you focus attention on the upper half of a scene, whereas a different subgroup activates when attention is transferred to the lower half. They were surprised to see the pattern of activity among the neurons that process the lower half of the visual field echoed the behavior of the cells for the field's upper half. It showed that while you are consciously tuning for a particular shape or color—say, your lost keys—in one part of your visual field, you may be subconsciously alerting the entire visual system to that pattern for a more efficient search.

Now all you have to do is remember to leave the keys out where you can see them.

Part 2

Engaging the World

Getting Out and About

9 A.M. to Noon

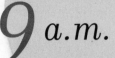

9 a.m.

Encountering Others

As you leave your home, you spot someone a block away and instantly recognize your neighbor. You smile at a young mother pushing a baby stroller, frown when a shabbily dressed stranger crosses your path, and can tell instantly when you arrive at work if your boss is in a bad mood.

That's an aspect of social cognition, and it's an amazing skill. All human faces look pretty much alike, when you come right down to it. Yet most of us can pick a familiar face out of a crowd in a microsecond and know if the person is friend or foe and what kind of mood he or she is in.

You know who you know and who you don't, and you know what these people are thinking and feeling. So how does your brain do this?

That Face, That Familiar Face

Neuroscientists don't have all the details about how we recognize people we've seen before or know, but some say they have a good idea where it lives. They say there is a specific ID center for faces in a visual processing center of the brain called the fusiform face area (FFA): a pea-sized region located in the fusiform gyrus, a spindle-shaped area where the temporal lobes meet the occipital lobe.

The fusiform gyrus is known to help process color information and word and number recognition, as well as recognizing faces, bodies, and objects. The FFA appears to be a subsection specifically dedicated to recognizing human faces: when brains were imaged with functional magnetic resonance imaging (fMRI), this area lit up when they viewed human faces.

We're not born with that ability fully developed: fMRIs show the FFA is larger in adults than in children and that it grows as children age, along with an improved memory for faces. Very young babies know their mothers but may not recognize other people when presented in differing situations. This may explain why tiny children who greet you with joy one day may shriek with fear if you next appear with a different hair style or hair color or in an unexpected setting. Research also shows we are much more adept at recognizing faces of our own race and that aging, disease, and mental illness can affect the FFA (see "Are You My Mother?" on the following page). The fusiform gyrus is less developed in those with schizophrenia and autism (see "The Broken Mirror," page 52).

Scientists aren't in complete agreement about face detection in the FFA. Some say neurons in the FFA work the same as other brain neurons to distinguish objects, except that those in the FFA are more attuned to facial details because of experience viewing human faces. Another group of vision experts questions the existence of a specific face-detection center altogether, arguing that the process of seeing many faces trains the general object recognition part of your brain to recognize specific ones.

The most current thought is that face recognition, along with almost all other brain functions, involves many brain processes that overlap and support one another.

Friend or Foe? Read My Face

When you got to work, it didn't take very long for you to figure out that a coworker is really mad at you. You can tell just by looking at him. And you could tell that the woman sitting across from you on the bus this morning was grieving, though neither of them said a word.

It happens without even thinking about it, whether you and the face you're looking at is in Topeka or Timbuktu. Human expressions appear to be universal and universally understood across cultures and

ARE YOU MY MOTHER?

Some people can't recognize faces at all, even those of close relatives and friends. They have been known to walk right past their own mother without recognizing her when in an unfamiliar place.

The name for this is *prosopagnosia,* or face blindness. It's estimated that between 2 and 3 percent of all people are born with this condition, which is thought to be the result of problems in the right fusiform gyrus—that face place in the brain. It can also be caused by brain injury or disease in that area. Prosopagnosia can't be cured, but people with this condition can learn other ways of recognizing people, such as by hair color or style, gait, and speech patterns.

In another condition related to recognition, Capgras's syndrome, people recognize others but have no emotional connection. They believe a loved one has been replaced by an imposter. The syndrome can be caused by illness, damage to the temporal lobe, dementia, or schizophrenia.

races. Paul Ekman, psychology professor emeritus at the University of California, San Francisco, has spent forty years studying human facial expressions. He's catalogued more than ten thousand possible combinations of facial muscle movements and what they mean. Ekman's research has convinced him (and others) that the language of the face has biological origins and that culture has no significant effect on it. In other words, expressions are the same the world over, and we "read" them no matter where we are.

And it's a good thing: at times, our very survival depends on being able to read others' faces and tell if someone is a friend or foe. Take that shabbily dressed man approaching you on the street. Visual signals are shunted from your optic nerve and the occipital lobe to other parts of the brain for processing: the ever-vigilant amygdala and the forebrain, which handles conscious thoughts and decisions. The hair-triggered amygdala makes a split-second decision about friend or foe. Then the thinking brain checks in to assess the situation and you realize it's a local laborer, not a deranged assassin.

Psychologists have been researching social perception for decades, but only recently have brain imaging and other techniques begun to explain how it works in the brain. They find that your thinking brain may have to work to overcome biases and emotional responses. We respond more positively to beauty, for example, especially to child-like features on an adult woman and to people of our own race. If the stranger is unattractive, of a different race, and angry, your amygdala will be on alert. In fact, studies show that it reacts more strongly to an angry face than to a snake.

Not surprisingly, women are better at social perception than men are. It's not your imagination: women have a better memory for faces than men do. A Swedish team of psychologists showed that women are better on average than men at remembering faces, particularly female faces. One reason is that females may have an advantage when it comes to episodic memory, a type of long-term memory based on personal experiences. Previous studies have also shown that women have a better memory for verbal information, which they may use to dissect a person's underlying motives or intentions—a skill that seems to elude many men.

Mirror, Mirror: Copycat Neurons in the Brain

You've never set up a PowerPoint presentation, so your coworker is demonstrating it to you step-by-step. Last night at the gym, an instructor showed you how to move into a yoga asana by doing it first and this morning you showed your three-year-old how to tie a shoe lace.

It's true what they say: we learn by imitation, and scientists discovered why a decade or so ago. They found we all have what they call mirror neurons: neurons scattered throughout key parts of our brain that fire as we perform an action and also fire when we watch someone else perform that same action. They discovered that these same neurons fire when we just *think* about performing that action, as though we are rehearsing it in our minds. In animal studies, researchers found that mirror neurons in monkeys even fired when they just heard someone performing an action they had experienced.

These neurons are found in areas associated with movement and perception, as well as in the regions that correspond to language and understanding someone else's feelings and intentions: the premotor cortex, the inferior and posterior parietal lobe, the superior temporal sulcus, and the insula.

The findings go a long way toward explaining a biological basis for empathy, for example, and for learning motor and language skills and explaining the basis of some social and psychological problems. Mirror neurons might contribute to the influence of violent video games as well. Studies show that games that allow us to imitate violence may reinforce pleasure associated with inflicting harm.

And low mirror neuron activity is common in people with autism, which is thought to be due in part at least to flaws in the mirror neuron system.

The Broken Mirror: Autism Insights from Mirror Neurons and Face Perception

Autism (from the Greek word *autos,* meaning "self") is a condition of near-isolation and social withdrawal that usually shows up in early childhood. Those with autism often have difficulty understanding what others are feeling and thinking. They also can have problems with movement, language, and recognizing others.

Experts aren't sure what causes autism. It's known to be a brain disorder with a strong genetic component. Studies are showing that those with autism have abnormalities in specific brain areas, including those for facial recognition and mirror neurons—areas that are essential in relating to others.

In a recent international study, a group of researchers, noting that activity in the fusiform gyrus face recognition area was lower in people with autism, autopsied the brains of seven children and adults who had had autism and compared them to ten normal brains. They found that the visual cortex and the cerebral cortex of those with autism appear normal, but they also found significantly lowered neuron density and numbers in the fusiform gyrus.

Another study at Harvard Medical School looked at mirror neurons and concluded they fired much less often in autistic children when they watched someone else make meaningless finger movements compared to the neural activity in nonautistic kids. That lack of response could reflect a failure of mirror neurons' most basic function: recognizing others' actions.

In another study, researchers showed pictures of people with distinctive facial expressions to autistic and nonautistic teens. Both groups could imitate the expressions and say what emotions they expressed. But only the nonautistic teens showed activity in mirror neurons corresponding to the emotions.

TIP-OF-THE-TONGUE MOMENTS

We all know the maddening experience of not being able to think of a certain word that is undoubtedly somewhere in our brain. It could be because you're, well, getting older or, research suggests, because you just haven't used that word very often.

Researchers have discovered an association between a specific region in the brain's language system and these tip-of-the-tongue (TOT) experiences, which are a normal part of aging. Deborah Burke of Pomona College and her team found that TOT moments became more frequent as gray matter density in the left insula declined. This area of the brain has been implicated in sound processing and production. The findings support a model proposed by Burke and her colleagues, which predicts that when we do not often use a word, the connections among all its various representations in the brain become weak.

"Words aren't stored as a unit," Burke says. "Instead you have the sound information connected to semantic information, connected to grammatical information, and so on. But the sounds are much more vulnerable to decay over time than other kinds of information, and that leads to the TOT experience."

These studies don't explain the full range of autism symptoms, but they give more insight into the difficulties of living with autism and the brain areas that appear responsible.

IF I COULD READ YOUR MIND . . .

We do read each other's minds in some way, and all day long. Social interactions are based on our perceptions of what others are thinking, as well as their actions. We interpret others' behavior based on what we think is going on in their minds, and we predict their behavior—and modify our own behavior—based on this understanding. We appear to do this in a part of the brain called the temporoparietal junction (TPJ), according to research by Rebecca Saxe at the Massachusetts Institute of Technology. The TPJ sits between the temporal lobes (involved in speech, memory, and hearing) and the parietal lobes (which integrate sensory input). Functional magnetic resonance imaging (fMRI) has shown increased activity in the junction when people think about other people's thoughts.

The research is part of what is called theory of mind: the ability to attribute thoughts and feelings to others as well as ourselves and to know the difference and to understand and predict behaviors. It's a hot area, and scientists are imaging, theorizing, and arguing about where in the mind (and how) we make judgments about others as opposed to inanimate objects, how we reach moral decisions, and how we generally make decisions about social interaction.

---

10 a.m.

Peak Performance— or Stress?

The phone is ringing, and no one is picking it up. You're on the other line, and two people are waiting by your desk, papers in hand. E-mail is blinking, and you are already five minutes overdue for a conference with your boss to explain why the project is running late and over budget.

You didn't even have to leave home to get stressed. A broken refrigerator, a dead car battery, a computer crash, a meltdown by your five-year-old, sharp words with your partner. Even the mere anticipation of stress can set us off.

It doesn't really much matter what is happening. What matters is how your hypothalamus is responding.

Stress in the Brain

For most early risers, midmorning is peak performance time—or is that peak stress time?

Stress is defined as an inability to cope with the demands or challenges presented to us. The stress response is your brain's attempt to try to establish balance with a powerful biological reaction. It's a survival skill that harkens back to the days when a quick response was vital to flee predators or fight for your life.

But it has become misplaced. Today our brain sets off those same alarms when we face mental or emotional stress. When your senses or neocortex register something indicating stress, the hypothalamus pops into action. It sets off a chain reaction involving the amygdala and the pituitary and adrenal glands, carried out by nerve impulses and an avalanche of hormones and neurotransmitters.

The adrenal glands send out epinephrine (better known as adrenaline) and the glucocorticoid cortisol. These chemical generals mobilize energy for muscles, increase cardiovascular tone so oxygen can travel more quickly, and temporarily turn off nonessential activities such as growth.

The Alarm That Doesn't Stop: Why Chronic Stress Is So Bad

Stress chemicals in your brain are gearing you up and perking you up. So this is good, right? Not so fast.

Activating the fight-or-flight system is an expensive operation for your body. It's so costly that it should be a rare and drastic event. It makes sense when the stressor is a war zone, a mountain lion attack, or an earthquake, flood, or fire.

But for most of us, a trip down the road to overload doesn't usually involve a major disaster. It's more likely to be set off by our reaction to day-to-day events that pile up beyond our ability to cope. The small stuff of everyday life can trigger a big response, and in some people it can set in motion a stress cycle as damaging in the long run as a major accident. It puts miles on our organs and kills off brain cells.

An occasional stress response is not bad. It can recharge you, get your system zinging, and give life a bit of zest. But habitual stress just wears you down. Like chronic pain, chronic stress is an alarm that doesn't shut off. Its incessant ringing eventually changes your mind and body.

Stress Destroys Neurons

While you are rushing to meet a deadline, anxiety vibrating through your brain, consider how unproductive mental stress is to your mental work.

Stress is a killer for brain cells. At least in rats, it may take only a single socially stressful situation to destroy newly created neurons in the hippocampus, the brain region involved in memory and emotion.

New nerve cells are continually generated in the hippocampus, where they are essential for learning. Scientists have long known that chronic stress can inhibit this neurogenesis (that is, nerve growth) and lead to depression. Daniel Peterson and his colleagues at the Rosalind Franklin University of Medicine and Science wanted to find out how the brain reacted to just a single stressful episode.

The team placed a young adult rat in a cage with two older rats that quickly attacked the newcomer. When they removed the younger animal twenty minutes later, they found that its stress hormone levels were six times as high as those of rats that had not experienced the terrifying encounter. Examining the young rat's brain, they saw that it had produced as many new neurons as its unstressed counterparts. Yet when they repeated the experiment with different rats and examined those brains a week after the incident, only a third of newly generated cells had survived.

Stress Ups the Risk of Alzheimer's Disease

Evidence is mounting that chronic stressors such as anxiety or fear can make the brain more susceptible to Alzheimer's disease.

A team at the Salk Institute for Biological Studies in La Jolla, California, stressed mice by physically restraining them for half an hour. The brief incident modified the tau protein, a key event in the development of Alzheimer's disease. Healthy tau supports neuron activity, but modified tau is believed to contribute to brain tangles associated with the disease.

After a single stress episode, tau morphed back to its original state within ninety minutes. But when the animals were stressed every day for two weeks, tau remained in its modified state long enough to allow the individual protein molecules to clump together: a first step toward neurofibrillary tangles, one of the hallmarks of Alzheimer's disease, says Robert A. Rissman, lead author of the study.

It may be that simply being prone to worry and tension can cause memory problems in old age, a human study shows. Looking at stress in humans, Robert Wilson and his colleagues at Rush University Medical Center in Chicago surveyed the stress susceptibility of more than a thousand elderly people over twelve years by rating their agreement with statements such as, "I am often tense and jittery." Volunteers who were anxiety prone had a 40 percent higher risk of developing mild cognitive impairment than more easygoing individuals.

Mild cognitive impairment—problems with mental functions not serious enough to interfere with daily functioning but enough to be noticeable—is thought to be a precursor for Alzheimer's disease. While brain autopsies did not turn up evidence of Alzheimer's disease in this group, the researchers think it's possible that the gradual compromising of memory systems creates vulnerability to the physical changes in the brain associated with the disease.

The Very Thought of It Is Enough

Curse the imagination. Our stress response can be set in motion not only by an actual event like a chewing out by the boss, but by mere anticipation of it. This can be useful when it's appropriate to the situation, such as when you are walking alone down a dark, deserted street. It's good to be on guard then.

But when you are chronically anticipating danger that doesn't come, you've moved from alertness to anxiety, neurosis, and even paranoia, says stress expert and Stanford University professor Robert Sapolsky. And anxiety rips up your limbic system, especially your inner sentry, the amygdala, which gets these anticipatory or abstract messages confused with real sensory data. An angry face can set it off as well as an angry action—and, it seems, just the thought of an angry action. Since much of this information is subliminal and preconscious, your amygdala can be activated before you know it consciously.

SEVEN BAD THINGS STRESS DOES TO YOU AND YOUR BRAIN

If you need reasons to lower stress, consider this: stress left turned on high wears you down like tires spinning on a slick road. That's just the body. Here's what research says about your brain on stress:

- Kills off newly formed brain cells
- Contributes to depression (and just about every organ disease)
- Makes you more vulnerable to Alzheimer's disease and dementia
- Inhibits the formation of memories in the hippocampus
- Damages the prefrontal cortex, which houses executive functions that help us reason, set goals, and make decisions. (See "11 A.M.")
- Impedes memory-related functions such as test taking
- Sets up a system for generalized anxiety

Multitasking—Again?

By 10:30 A.M. or so, you're coping with the morning overload by doubling or even tripling up on the tasks. We all do it the time: talking on the phone while keyboarding, driving, folding laundry, cooking, reading e-mail, scanning articles (you're probably doing it right now). Walking and chewing gum may work for you in the short run, but studies show you can strain your brain—or, more precisely, your attention resources and memory—when you try to multitask, a practice common in office, home, and commuting cars.

Not only is it inefficient. Its stress can hurt your hippocampus (the place where memories are formed) and your prefrontal cortex (where executive decisions are made). That damage can make it difficult to learn new facts and skills, and it can even provoke an attack of pseudo attention deficit disorder (ADD), in which we constantly seek new information but have difficulties in concentrating on its content—no news to most of us who multitask madly with e-mail, phone, and text messaging.

The Limits of Multitasking

A growing number of studies show that trying to juggle several jobs rather than finishing them one at a time can take longer overall and leave multitaskers with a reduced ability to perform each task. The combination results in inefficiency, sloppy thinking, and mistakes—not to mention the possible dangers of divided attention for drivers, air traffic controllers, doctors, and parents of small children.

It's been known since the 1930s that processing the information for one task can cause interference with another. Your brain loves auto-pilot, which takes a lot less energy. So it performs automated processes quickly and unconsciously, and sometimes we have trouble suppressing them when we want to. For example, as soon as we see a word, we decipher it unconsciously. Interference can result if the word's meaning contradicts other information provided simultaneously. When participants in a study were asked to name the color of a word, such as *green,* that was printed in an incompatible color—say, red—they experienced difficulty saying the color. The two tasks got tangled: the brain must suppress one that has been learned so well that it has become automatic (reading) to attend to a second that requires concentration (naming the color).

Scientists believe it's not possible for the brain to carry out two or more processes simultaneously. Up to a point, people can improve their multitasking skills with practice—at least those that can become routine. The brain simply automates some and pays less attention to it. Some scientists theorize that the brain pays attention in three-second bursts—somewhat akin to channel surfing, and about as efficient.

In one magnetic resonance imaging (MRI) study of multitasking brains, research teams at the Center for Cognitive Brain Imaging at Carnegie Mellon University were struck by how overall brain activity dropped when people tried to perform two tasks. The activity was less than two-thirds as much as the total devoted to each task when processed independently.

How Your Brain Helps Your Job Kill You

Okay, you're convinced: stress is bad. But maybe you didn't know it's worse than unhealthy living. Directly and indirectly, it may be the single worst thing your brain does to your heart.

According to a recent British study, living in constant fight-or-flight mode contributes to direct biological wear and tear and accounts for two-thirds of the risk for heart disease. The other third stems from

---

FIGHTING FIRE WITH FIRE:
USING STRESS HORMONES TO LOWER STRESS

Cortisol, a hormone secreted by the adrenal glands in times of stress, has a bad reputation. Most studies have looked at the hormone's long-term negative effects when chronic stress keeps its levels high. But it seems that a stiff jolt just before a stressful situation can help the brain reduce negative effects.

Psychologists Oliver T. Wolf and Serkan Het of Bielefeld University in Germany gave twenty-two young women thirty milligrams of cortisol—a fairly high dose—and a control group of twenty-two women a placebo. Then they stressed both groups: the women were asked to give a speech in a fake job interview and to count backward by seventeens from a large number, all the while being monitored by stern-faced examiners and videotaped. The women who got cortisol reported less negative effect after the stress test.

Exactly how cortisol provided this protection isn't known. But it is known to be active in several brain regions that modulate emotions. It might interfere with retrieving emotional memories, so unpleasant experiences aren't recalled very well. If this is true, it could point the way toward using cortisol to treat people who have survived terrible events and suffer from posttraumatic stress disorder.

stress-related unhealthy behaviors, such as poor diet, smoking, and lack of exercise, as well as lifestyle-influenced conditions such as high blood pressure and blood glucose.

The finding comes from a large long-term project, the Whitehall Study, begun in the early 1970s to track eighteen thousand male British civil servants. It found that the lowest-ranking white-collar workers had the highest rates of premature death—a surprise, because it turned out that workload or responsibility had little relation to stress levels. Rather, it was how much control employees had over the work they did and how they did it.

The follow-up Whitehall II study identified what twenty years of that stress did to the subjects' hearts. In 2008, researchers found that workers with the highest stress levels had the lowest heart rate variability, a measure of heart rhythms controlled by the body's autonomic nervous system (our internal regulatory system). Chronic exposure to stress hormones weakens the heart's ability to respond to changing demands, and low heart rate variability is associated with greater risk of heart attack and lower survival rates afterward.

You Can Lull Your Brain Away from Stress

The good news is that stress can be controlled, or at least minimized, with medications, talk therapy, exercise, or stress reduction activities such as meditation and its cousins, yoga and tai chi.

Many people aren't helped by current medications, or they choose not to take them because of side effects. The nondrug therapies can help. The mind-body interaction and the relationship between stress and disease is old stuff. It's known that the brain and the immune system continuously signal each other, often along the same pathways, which may explain how state of mind affects health.

Studies show that thirty minutes of meditation a day can improve concentration and focus, and lower blood pressure and other symptoms of stress. (See "7:00 A.M.")

Music, performed or listened to, lowers stress. Radio station KDFC-FM in the San Francisco Bay Area advertises its classical music program as "an island of sanity," and for some it is. People play it to keep themselves calmer at work, home, or office.

Flow Versus Stress

When things are going really well, we call it flow. When they are snarled as badly as this morning's traffic, we call it stress.

Stimulation and challenge can be good for us and keep us alert and interested. A little moderate short-term stress sharpens memory and even our senses: taste buds, olfactory receptors, the cochlear cells in the ears. When we are under moderate stress, they all require less stimulation to get excited and pass information on to the brain. Indeed, there can be an almost ecstatic heightening of senses at times of great danger or stress. New activities, repeated into expertise, exercise our brain and promote the growth of new neurons.

Pressure ramped up to stress levels spurs neurons too—and then snips them dead. So far there is no generally accepted level at which stress is beneficial or becomes just too much. In the 1970s, psychologist Mihaly Csikszentmihályi coined the term *flow psychology* to describe the great absorption, focus, and enjoyment of the moment that results when there's a balance between our skills and the pressure and challenge of a situation. (Think of Tiger Woods sinking a putt in the last round of a championship game.) "It is how people respond to stress that determines whether they will profit from misfortune or be miserable," Csikszentmihályi wrote in *Flow: The Psychology of Optimal Experience.*

Music making is one of the flow experiences Csikszentmihályi describes, and a recent study suggests what might be happening in the brain at flow: it could be that an experience of flow dampens the self-censoring centers in the brain.

Jazz greats have said that spinning off an improvised tune is like entering another world. Researchers at the National Institutes of Health gave six professional jazz pianists a few days to memorize a tune new to them. The musicians then tickled the ivories while being scanned by an MRI machine, playing the novel composition, and then an improvisation in the same key.

The improvised jam provoked stronger activity in the medial pre-frontal cortex, a part of the brain active in autobiographical storytell-ing, among other varieties of self-expression. At the same time, activity dipped in the dorsolateral prefrontal cortex (an area linked to planning and self-censorship). That's similar to what happens during dreams, supporting the altered-state notion.

Researchers note that the same pattern might show up in all kinds of improvisations. It might also be what's happening when we are ex-periencing flow.

Decisions, Decisions, and More Decisions

You began making decisions, really, before you were even completely awake: Hit the snooze button, or roll out of bed? Shower or not? Black shoes or brown?

Right about now, approaching midday, you could be overwhelmed by choices. Your brain will have taken in and organized vast amounts of data, you will already have made literally thousands of decisions, large and small, and this will continue until your brain takes you into sleep again.

Life is jam-packed with choices and decisions. Most of them are trivial, but some, such as medical, financial, and moral decisions, are quite momentous. Researchers have long been interested in how your brain makes all these choices—in particular, how we make moral choices, especially when under stress—and in the role of intuition and the subconscious in choice. The subject and processes are complex, and researchers are discovering much about how our brains choose among variables. They are also discovering that contemplating options and making choices tires out our brain and makes thinking less effective, which could lead us to make worse decisions.

The Brain's CEO

The brain's choice-meister is often referred to as *executive function:* it has been compared to that of a company's chief executive officer.

Researchers don't agree yet about where exactly the CEO is in your brain, but they do agree that, like consciousness, it's probably in the frontal lobes. Its job is to coordinate the vast variety of incoming information into meaningful patterns and then coordinate the many brain activities we need to make decisions about these data. Among these actions are setting goals, making plans as to how to reach those goals, and being able to shift plans to meet changing situations.

The frontal lobes are sensitive to many kinds of brain injury and disease: people with autoimmune diseases often have some loss of executive function, as do those who undergo chemotherapy. The frontal lobes are also affected by mental disorders and substance abuse. And this damage may not show up or get diagnosed quickly. Even those who are seriously disabled by problems with executive function can appear normal under routine psychological and neurological tests.

"Chemo Brain" Can Ambush Your CEO

Cancer therapy can save your life, but it can also cause "chemo brain," the mental fogginess and memory and concentration problems that can persist for years after treatment has ended.

Researchers led by Michelle L. Monje of Harvard University have discovered why: the chemicals and radiation used to kill tumor cells damage the stem cell reservoir in the hippocampus and nearly halt the formation of new neurons. The hippocampus is vital for laying down new memories, and in healthy people, stem cells continue to add new circuits there, says Stanford University neuroscientist Theo D. Palmer, who worked with Monje.

The researchers found that radiation treatment also triggers a response from microglial cells, the immune cells of the central nervous system. Because inflammatory cells stifle neuronal growth, some experts think that the microglia may be the real culprit behind radiation-induced brain problems.

There is hope for those with this condition. The researchers' previous work in rats showed that anti-inflammatory drugs helped to restore some new neuron growth. Exercise has been shown to stimulate neurogenesis in healthy animals and in people, so Monje thinks there is a good chance that being active would improve cognition in cancer survivors too.

Choosing Economically

Your brain, like any good consumer, is concerned with cost-effectiveness and the best allocation of resources. Making decisions is part of that neuroeconomic process. Our brains have evolved to capture, store, and process input and to make choices in the most economical way. Unfortunately, these decision-making programs can be hijacked, according to Michael Shermer, writing for *Scientific American.*

Oxytocin, the neurotransmitter of bonding and love, can affect decision making by making us more trusting—sometimes too trusting. Addictive drugs rewire the brain's dopamine system, which is normally

---

DOES PRICE AFFECT YOUR WINE CHOICE? YOU BETCHA

It's all about neuroeconomics: our brain seems to equate price with pleasure. Wine tastes better when we think it costs more money, says Antonio Rangel of the California Institute of Technology, an author of a wine-tasting study.

Twenty volunteers had their brains scanned using functional magnetic resonance imaging (fMRI) while they tasted five supposedly different cabernet sauvignons, each identified by a different price. In fact, there were only three different wines, and two of them were presented twice: once at a high price and once at a low price.

The trick worked as expected. The volunteers rated the wines according to their stated price: the "cheapest" tasted cheap, and the most "expensive" was everybody's favorite. But not only did the wine tasters report they liked the pricier choices better, their brains showed an increase in activity in the medial orbitofrontal cortex, an area of the brain that previous studies suggest might encode for the pleasantness of an experience.

used to reward choices that are good for us, such as obtaining food, family, and friends, to reward choosing the next drug high instead.

Ideas can do something similar, says Shermer. They can take over the role of reward signals that feed into the dopamine neurons. This effect includes bad ideas, that is, ideas bad for the people acting on them, "such as the Heaven's Gate cult members who chose suicide to join the mother ship they believed was awaiting them near Comet Hale-Bopp. The brains of suicide bombers have been similarly commandeered by bad ideas from their religions or politics," he says, writing in *Scientific American*.

Making an Emotional Moral Choice

Would you take one human life to save many? The obvious answer might seem to be yes—but what if your choice meant you would sacrifice your own child?

For the past decade or so, cognitive scientists have been examining what happens in the brain when we struggle with moral and ethical decisions. A paper in *Nature* examined this question by comparing moral judgments made by neurologically normal people with those made by people with damage to a brain area known to be active in moral sentiments such as compassion, guilt, and shame—the ventromedial prefrontal cortex (VMPFC).

The study found that people with VMPFC damage were more likely to make utilitarian choices in moral dilemmas—judgments that favor the greater good or the welfare of many over the welfare of fewer individuals. VMPFC patients, for instance, were more likely to say it was okay to push someone in front of a moving train if you knew the resulting stoppage would save the lives of five workers down the track.

In another study, people with damage to the VMPFC were asked to respond to a variety of hypothetical moral dilemmas with emotional components of different strengths, and their responses were compared with those of people whose forebrains were intact. This study also showed utilitarian choices in those with forebrain damage. For example, many of them said they would smother their own baby to save a group of other people, but those with intact forebrains more often said they would not do so.

Choosing Wearies Your Brain

Cheesecake, apple pie, or chocolate decadence cake? Having too many choices may seem like a good thing, but it sure can be tiring. And like an overworked muscle, a tired brain is less effective.

A clutch of studies shows that people faced with many choices lose focus and later find it hard to make subsequent choices, even if they've been participating in something seemingly fun, like choosing gifts for a wedding registry. One study looked at several situations involving about four hundred people and choice making. In some cases, they were asked to choose; in another case, they simply had to contemplate the options. University of Minnesota psychologist Kathleen Vohs and colleagues found that those who had been busy making choices performed worse on math tests afterward, compared to those who looked at options without making a choice. Making decisions seemed to deplete mental energy, said Vohs.

In the past, researchers studying actions that tire the brain's executive functions focused on activities that involved exertion of self-control or the regulation of attention. These more recent study results suggest that taxing mental activities may actually be much broader in scope and affect both commitment and trade-off resolutions. For commitment, the brain has to switch from a state of deliberation to one of implementation. In other words, you have to make a transition from thinking about options to following through on a decision. This switch, according to Vohs, requires executive resources.

Moreover, the mere act of resolving trade-offs may wear your brain out, according to an investigation by Yale University professor Nathan Novemsky and his colleagues. In one study, the scientists showed that people who only had to rate the appeal of different options were much less depleted than those who had to make choices among the same options.

These findings have important implications. If making choices depletes your brain's executive resources, then decisions downstream might not be optimal when we're forced to choose with a fatigued brain.

Indeed, University of Maryland psychologist Anastasiya Pocheptsova and colleagues found exactly this effect: those who had to regulate their attention, which requires executive control, made significantly different choices from people who did not. These different choices followed a specific pattern. People became reliant on what the researchers called a more simplistic and often inferior thought process and were vulnerable to "perceptual decoys." For example, participants were asked to ignore interesting subtitles as they watched an otherwise boring film clip. When they were then presented with choices, they were much more likely to choose an option that stood next to a clearly inferior "decoy"—an option that was similar to one of the good choices but was obviously not quite as good. Participants who watched the same clip but were not asked to ignore anything weren't as vulnerable to decoys.

It seems that trying to ignore an interesting item just plain exhausted the limited resources of the executive functions, which leads to this good advice: take this into account when making decisions. If you've just spent lots of time focusing on a particular task, exercising self-control, or making lots of seemingly minor choices, then you probably shouldn't try to make a major decision.

The Brain Has a Section for Regret

So you went for the cheesecake for your late morning break, and now you're sorry. You really wanted that chocolate.

It's human nature to sometimes regret a decision: your medial orbitofrontal cortex (OFC) and some French researchers know all about that feeling of remorse. Giorgio Coricelli and his colleagues at the Institute of Cognitive Sciences at the National Science Research Center in Bron, France, used fMRI scans to monitor how people make decisions and how they feel about them after the fact. The team presented volunteers with two choices, one of which carried higher risk than the other but had the potential for greater reward as well. After choosing, the volunteers were told the outcome of their decision. In some cases, the researchers also revealed what would have happened if they had made a different choice. Learning that the choice not taken was better than the one they chose was strongly correlated with activity in the medial OFC, which sits above the orbits of the eyes in the brain's frontal lobe.

The amount of OFC activity was tied to the level of regret, and that in turn corresponded to the difference between the result of the selected choice and that of the alternative outcome. But when there was no choice—when participants were assigned one of two possibilities and felt no control over the outcomes—there was no remorse activity in the brain at the results. This suggests that a feeling of personal responsibility is involved in feelings of regret. This may not be such a good thing, since people who don't feel regret may not be able to change their behavior to avoid other situations that would end with regret.

Like choosing that cheesecake.

12 noon

The Hungry Brain

You can tell it's time for lunch: you just inadvertently deleted the letter you've been working on for the past hour.

It's been a long, hard morning, and you never did get a good breakfast. With your blood sugar plummeting and your serotonin running on empty, you're having trouble concentrating and your brain is getting cranky. Looks like you need to feed your amygdala and hypothalamus.

We need to eat, of course. The old wives tale about low blood sugar contributing to groggy thinking and bad moods is not only true; it's been joined by evidence that low serotonin can make us *really* cranky. We need to eat to get the fuel (glucose) and building blocks (essential amino acids) to keep us not only alive but on an even emotional keel. (See "7:00 A.M.")

How Hunger Works in Your Brain

Hunger tells us when we need to eat, and a handy thing it is. Hunger (or appetite) is a multifaceted function, involving hormones in your stomach lining, your ever-active amygdala, and a control section in the hypothalamus called the arcuate nucleus.

The arcuate nucleus regulates your appetite by counting calories for you—sort of. It monitors your blood levels of glucose and insulin and the hormones ghrelin and leptin to see if your body has enough calories and nutrients. Ghrelin, produced in cells lining the stomach, stimulates appetite: ghrelin levels rise before meals and fade after you've eaten. Its counterpart, the hormone leptin (mostly produced from fat tissue), puts the brakes on appetite after you've eaten—most of the time. Various nerves and stomach chemicals report directly to satiety centers in the brain stem called the nucleus tractus solitarus.

The arcuate nucleus adjusts your appetite, and some of its neurons can upset all those diet plans. They contain a substance, neuropeptide Y (NPY), that influences hunger. When activated, these neurons can stimulate what amounts to eating binges that empty your fridge and pack on the pounds. There are other pitfalls that can throw off your appetite regulator, including the amygdala.

We're Losing Our Scents

Did you have trouble detecting the smell and taste of herbs in your luncheon salad dressing? It's possible: that powerful sense and your serviceable olfactory receptors are gradually fading away.

We've actually been losing functional olfactory receptors for a long time, even before we humans diverged from other primates. In analyzing genetic sequences of different species, researchers at Rockefeller University and Duke University have found that compared with mice, rats, dogs, and other primates, people have a greater percentage of pseudogenes—defunct genes that arise through mutation—littering our olfactory genome.

No one knows why human olfaction has been circling the evolutionary drain. Most likely, somewhere along the line, smell became less relevant to our survival and reproduction. One hypothesis is that improvements in eyesight shifted reliance away from our noses and to our eyes. Yoav Gilad of the University of Chicago and colleagues have shown that the gradual deterioration of functional olfactory receptors paralleled the acquisition of trichromatic (full-color) vision in humans and other primates. If sight replaced smell, it might have affected many aspects of living, including foraging, courting, and detecting predators, they speculate.

Others speculate that evolution into upright walking brought our heads up, reducing the amount of time spent sniffing around on the ground for food. Better verbal communication or improved intelligence may have also reduced the reliance on olfaction.

Still, the average human nose can detect some ten thousand odors. Not bad.

Still Hungry? When Hunger Goes Awry

You ate lunch, a big lunch. You had dessert too—the chocolate cake this time. But you're still hungry, or your amygdala is telling you that you are, even when your frontal lobes know you've really had enough. Could it be that you are addicted to food?

Food is a basic survival need, but overeating isn't. It's an addiction and very like drug addiction, which may explain why so many of us have such trouble with weight.

Scientists are finding overeating operates in the brain much the same as addictive drugs do. Your amygdala (once again!) is part of the problem. It's always on the lookout for your survival, and that includes food. It sends out signals when it sees something it has been trained to regard as important to your survival, such as a dangerous predator or a hot meatball sandwich.

Researchers using fMRI imaging have found that the amygdala lights up in the brains of hungry people when they see anything edible. Similarly, imaging shows that the brain's reward center (the nucleus accumbens) is flooded with dopamine when you see something delicious. That's very like what some experiments with cocaine addicts show: when they saw lines of white powder, their amygdalas perked right up, and dopamine flushed the nucleus accumbens.

After you have eaten, the amygdala no longer responds to food for awhile—usually. But when your dopamine levels are off, the eating urge continues. Overeating can become an addiction.

If you're already overweight, you're at higher risk. An experiment by the National Institute on Drug Abuse found the number of dopamine receptors in overweight people is closely related to BMI (body mass index): the higher the BMI, the heavier you are, and the fewer dopamine receptors you have. The researchers concluded that very overweight people have a dopamine shortage, which makes them constantly seek reward stimulants in the form of food. This sets up a vicious cycle that's similar to dopamine seeking in drug addicts: an addict's brain notes the dopamine surge, then compensates for the excess dopamine by reducing the number of dopamine receptors, which triggers a need for more dopamine.

These experiments support the theory that the brain's yen for food and drug addiction are very much the same and that similar medications and behavioral control might play a role in controlling both kinds of addictions.

Why Calories Taste Delicious

There's something inherently pleasurable about eating food with calories. And our brain knows which food that is: sugar—which as we know all too well is high in calories—is still pleasurable even when it isn't sweet, a rodent study shows.

It's thought that two brain mechanisms control our food intake. The hypothalamus tells us when we need to eat to maintain our body weight "set point," much like a thermostat set on a specific temperature. Other brain centers such as the dopamine reward system control our desire to eat. When you covet a bowl of chocolate ice cream after dinner—a food that you don't *need* to eat but *want* to eat—it's your dopamine reward system getting excited.

This desire to eat can lead us crave tasty foods even when not hungry, contributing to obesity. When you're very hungry, you seek out food with lots of calories. But does your dopamine reward system care about calories or is it just concerned with taste and pleasure?

Neuroscientist Ivan de Araujo (now at the John Pierce Laboratory affiliated with Yale University) and colleagues at Duke University put this question to a line of mice genetically engineered to be unable to detect the taste of sweetness. Therefore, in these mice, any change in reward behavior would not be connected with taste or sweetness. If these mice prefer sweetness, it would be because sweeter foods have more calories, researchers reasoned.

In the first experiments, the genetically altered mice were completely uninterested in the "sweet" rewarding properties of sucrose (table sugar) and showed no preference for sucrose over plain water. In contrast, mice without the genetic mutation strongly preferred the sucrose solution.

The scientists then conditioned the genetically altered mice to associate the sweet solutions with higher calories. Although they still couldn't taste the sweetness, they learned to relate the taste with higher calories, and to prefer that solution.

Finally, the experiments were then repeated with sucralose, an artificial sweetener that tastes sweet but contains no calories. The normal mice lapped up the sucralose—but the genetically altered mice did not.

The researchers then determined that calories (and not the taste of sweetness) were triggering the dopamine reward system. They used a technique known as in vivo microdialysis to show that calorie consumption increases dopamine levels in the nucleus accumbens, regardless of taste, in genetically altered mice. Again, normal mice had a dopamine surge with real and fake sugar, but genetically altered mice only showed an increase in dopamine with the real thing.

This raises may questions. How does the dopamine system sense calories? Does the same phenomenon occur when calories come from different food types, such as fat? And does this apply to humans?

And it gives an important clue to the rise of obesity and to how your brain controls eating behavior.

Addicted to _____ (Fill in the Blank)

You've probably suspected that addiction is not limited to drugs, smoking, and alcohol. Many interlocking and overlapping brain parts get turned on by—well, by just about anything.

In addition to the usual physical suspects, you can get hooked on a feeling as well, and that includes (but apparently isn't limited to) compulsive behavior such as gambling, shopping, obsessive Internet use, television viewing, risk taking, eating, and sex. (Orgasm has actually been described as the biggest legal high you can experience without a prescription. See "10:00 P.M.")

That's because these feelings, thoughts, and sensations kidnap and convert what scientists tantalizingly refer to as our reward system: a pleasure center your brain uses to decide what it likes and to then reward you for it with a burst of feel-good dopamine. It sounds at first as if it's a G spot for the brain: one neat little brain dot for registering pleasure, much like the so-called secret orgasmic spot in a woman. But while much is still being discovered about how the reward pathways work, scientists do know that your brain has multiple pleasure and reward centers and systems to register good things. And those are just about anything your brain decides is good.

Not surprisingly, the reward system is focused in your emotional brain in the limbic system and in its reaction to stimuli. Your amygdala helps decide whether an experience is pleasurable or bad and whether it should be repeated or avoided, and it sends that message along to the hippocampus, which helps record memories of the event, including where and when and with whom it happened. Eventually your thinking brain in the frontal regions of the cerebral cortex will coordinate and process all this information and decide how you'll respond.

Meanwhile, long neurons in the ventral tegmental area (VTA) near the base of your brain are sending dopamine to a structure deep beneath your frontal cortex called the nucleus accumbens. This pathway (the VTA-accumbens pathway) evaluates how good the experience is and sends that rating along to other parts of your reward circuit, including your amygdala and prefrontal cortex. The more rewarding the experience is, the more likely your brain is to want to repeat it.

Certainly many events and experiences register pleasure, but some things are more potent than others. All drugs of potential abuse, for example, prompt a veritable tsunami of dopamine—a reaction much more powerful than any natural reward. Eventually these reactions overwhelm, capture, and change the reward pathway, leaving us craving more and more. (See "6:00 P.M.")

Scientists continue to discover many chemicals and processes involved in addiction and in pleasure, looking for both information about the ways we are driven to seek rewards and ways to help treat addictions when enough is too much.

Self-Control Sucks Your Energy

Well, no wonder you're hungry. Now we know why: your brain is sucking the strength right out of you, and it's all because you've been good.

Day after day, you have struggled to control your irritation at the annoying behavior of a well-meaning friend. Suddenly, during a particularly grating encounter, you just blow up. You lose your temper out of all proportion to the event, and give your stunned friend a big piece of your mind.

It's a sorry lapse of willpower, and it might be connected to your glucose level. Such flare-ups are often related to how well you were holding down the hatch before it blew into the stratosphere. Scientists have discovered that not only does willpower have limits, it takes energy. Lots of it. A single brief act of self-control uses up some of your body's fuel and undermines your brain's ability to continue self-discipline.

Researchers at Florida State University asked volunteers to perform some mental tasks, such as ignoring a distracting stimulus while watching a video clip or suppressing racial stereotypes during a five-minute social interaction. It turns out these seemingly minor efforts depleted glucose in the bloodstream and affected volunteers' ability to maintain mental discipline during subsequent tasks.

When the study participants were given a sugar drink to boost their blood glucose levels, their performance returned to normal. But those who drank an artificially sweetened drink remained impaired.

"These findings show us that willpower is more than a metaphor," notes Matthew Gailliot, a graduate student in psychology who led the research. "It's metabolically expensive to maintain self-control."

Kathleen Vohs, a psychologist at the University of Minnesota who has studied choice (see "11:00 A.M."), found similar effects with self-control. Her research suggests that those who exercise self-control are more likely to make impulse purchases later—a finding that fits with the glucose depletion model. Moreover, self-control may be toughest for people whose bodies don't use blood glucose properly, such as those with type 2 diabetes. And these people can't benefit from the news that a sugar drink restores mental reserves.

Now these findings aren't a license to go on sugar benders in the name of willpower. But they do emphasize how metabolically expensive self-control can be. And why (gosh, it's your mom talking again) it's important to eat at mealtimes. Is that chocolate cake still around?

Yes, There Is Such a Thing as Brain Food

We all have bad brain days, when we mess up or muddle along in neutral. It's worse when we're running on empty, the way you probably were right before lunch.

Remember what an energy hog the brain is, burning through 20 percent of the body's metabolic fuel? Priming the brain with the right food can help us stay sharp. Research and observation show that what and when we eat can influence memory, learning, concentration, and decision making.

Your brain operates best when your blood glucose level is stable. Very high levels (such as in diabetes) interfere with mental function, and so do very low levels: when blood sugar drops, we fade.

You can help your brain avoid wild fluctuations by eating regular meals (or perhaps many small meals) throughout the day that are high in complex carbohydrates found in whole-grain products, legumes (beans), and vegetables. Lean protein found in meats, poultry, and fish helps stabilize glucose levels and boost attention, and the fatty acids found in fish oil lubricate your mental machinery (and your cardiovascular system). Vitamins and minerals found in food are also essential.

Fad diets that focus on one food type or group can wreak havoc by upsetting body and brain balance. Take protein-focused low-carbohydrate diets, for example. We need protein. Besides stabilizing blood sugar levels, protein contributes amino acids—the building material of much body chemistry, including hormones and neurotransmitters such as epinephrine and dopamine, which contribute to alertness. But paradoxically, high-protein meals have the opposite effect on tryptophan: they decrease brain levels of this amino acid needed to make serotonin, among other things. (Scientists aren't sure yet what that means; data on tryptophan and cognition are mixed.)

PROVISIONS FOR BRAIN POWER

A well-balanced diet benefits the brain just as it does the body. The table below highlights examples of the best brain foods (in **bold** type) and describes the functions of other nutrients found in foods that can influence concentration, memory, learning, and the overall health of the brain.

Nutrient	Function	Presence in Foods
Carbohydrates	Supply glucose for energy	Whole grains, fruits (especially **apples**), vegetables
Liquids	Stabilize circulation and nutrient transport, among other functions	Water, mineral water, unsweetened herbal and fruit teas
Caffeine, in small amounts	Dilates the blood vessels in the brain; increases concentration and memory	Coffee, black tea, **green tea**
Iron	Transports oxygen	Red meats, pumpkin seeds, sesame, soy flour, millet, poppy seeds, pine nuts, wheat germ, **oats,** dill, parsley, yeast, spinach, watercress, lentils, soybeans, white beans
Calcium	Conducts neuronal signals	Milk and milk products, poppy seeds, figs, sesame, soybeans, legumes, **nuts,** whole grains, wheat germ, oatmeal, broccoli, watercress, green vegetables, parsley
Zinc	Aids many chemical reactions in the brain; important for concentration and memory	Wheat germ, poppy seeds, sesame, pumpkin seeds, meat, eggs, milk, cheese, fish, carrots, whole-grain bread, potatoes
Phenylalanine, tyrosine	Act as precursors of epinephrine, norepinephrine, and dopamine; important for alertness and concentration	**Fish** (tuna, trout), meat, milk products, **soybeans,** cheese (cottage cheese), peanuts, wheat germ, almonds
Serine, methionine	Act as precursors of acetylcholine; essential for learning and memory formation	Fish, turkey, chicken, soybeans, beef, cashews, wheat germ, broccoli, peas, spinach, whole-grain bread, rice
Vitamin B$_1$ (thiamine)	Enables glucose metabolism; aids nerve cell function	Whole grains (wheat, spelt), oatmeal, wheat germ, sunflower seeds, legumes, nuts, pork
Unsaturated fatty acids, including omega-3 fatty acids	Build cell membranes	Fish, walnuts, spinach, corn oil, peanut oil, soybean oil, grape seed oil

Source: "Brain Food," *Scientific American Mind,* Oct.–Nov. 2007.

In short, a well-rounded diet helps maintain a well-balanced brain. And research continues to confirm that breakfast is the most important meal. Studies show that school-age children who eat breakfast score higher on tests and that school breakfast programs offered to kids who are severely undernourished improve their thinking and their school performance.

So what about lunch? Eat a low-calorie, protein-rich lunch that includes lots of vitamins and minerals—say, fish or chicken with a salad. This fuel will maintain attention and memory and minimize those afternoon energy dips. Save the pasta for dinnertime. Studies show that rice, noodle, and grain dishes boost blood tryptophan levels, which may hasten sleep.

YOUR APPETITE REGULATOR MIGHT BE REWRITABLE

Keeping a healthy weight is a struggle, especially as we get older. We all seem to have an individual body weight set point: a weight that is hardwired through sensitivity to leptin, the appetite-suppressing hormone. And we who diet know how hard it is to shift that point.

But there's evidence that leptin actually helps to write and rewrite the brain's appetite circuitry in the arcuate nucleus.

Researchers at Rockefeller and Yale universities found that the brains of obese, leptin-deficient mice have an appetite imbalance, with more connections to neurons that promote feeding and weight gain and fewer connections to appetite "stop" neurons than normal mice. Giving the mice leptin restored the balance of connections and reduced their appetite and weight; an appetite-stimulating hormone had the opposite effect.

A second team, from Oregon Health Sciences University, discovered that arcuate nucleus cells have fewer branchings in leptin-deficient mice. Giving them leptin just after birth mimicked a natural leptin surge and restored normal development. But giving leptin to adult mice had no effect on the number of branches, implying that leptin and nutrition during the first few weeks of life may have long-term effects on brain development.

Part 3

2
3
4

THE GUTS
OF THE DAY

GETTING DOWN

TO BUSINESS

1 P.M. TO 4 P.M.

The Tired Brain

As the after-lunch afternoon after-effect settles in, you might be feeling a bit brain-weary or just plain tired—in fact, very tired and even befuddled, and there are still workday hours left. But you can't seem to find your to-do list or remember what was on it. You're regretting that hearty pasta you just ate. Maybe, as Grandma used to say, all the blood has rushed from your brain to your belly to help digest that heavy lunch.

Or could it be your brain is feeling the effects of getting older? This is when those Alzheimer's disease fears creep in. But there's no reason to panic. If you're on the sunset side of fifty, it might just be normal aging in the brain.

Partial Recall: Why Memory Fades with Age

As we age, it becomes harder to recall names, dates, and even where we put our reading glasses. Chances are, memory is dulling just because your brain, like your body, is showing its age.

Researchers have pinned down some reasons for that loss. They find that the myelin (the brain's white matter) on bundles of axons—the projections sent out by neurons to signal other nerve cells—naturally erodes with age, disrupting communication, or cross talk, between brain areas. (See "6:00 A.M.")

Researchers at Harvard University, the University of Michigan at Ann Arbor, and Washington University in St. Louis gave a battery of cognitive tests and brain scans to ninety-three healthy volunteers, ages eighteen to ninety-three, in two age groups: one for ages eighteen to thirty-four and the other for ages sixty to ninety-three years. They were asked to perform several cognitive and memory exercises, such as determining whether certain words referred to living or nonliving objects. Researchers used functional magnetic resonance imaging (fMRI) to monitor activity in the fronts and backs of their brains to see if those areas were operating in sync. They found inner-brain communication had "dramatically declined" in the older group.

Further brain scans used a magnetic resonance imaging (MRI) technique that measures how well white matter is functioning by monitoring water movement. If neural communication is strong, water can be seen along the axonal bundles. If it's not, the image shows a scattered pattern. And that's what researchers saw in older group: an indication that their white matter had lost some of its integrity. The older groups' performance on memory and cognitive skill tests correlated with white matter loss: the seniors did poorly relative to their younger peers.

Also contributing to dimming skills is an age-related depletion of neurotransmitters and shrinking of actual nerve cell bodies and supporting cells. Sigh. Just like everything else in your body.

Can You Help Your Brain Stay Young(er)?

Experts say that using your brain keeps you from losing it, and they have evidence to back that up. There are numerous books, Web sites, and clinics offering such brain exercise programs, or you can try learning a new skill, honing an older one, staying social, and working out your body.

Physical exercise, it seems, builds new neurons in two brain areas, one of which is the dentate gyrus, a region in the hippocampus linked to age-related memory decline. (See "4:00 P.M.")

Several long-term studies also show the benefits of a circle of friends. One study followed more than two thousand women from the age of seventy-eight for four years and found that only 10 percent of those with a strong social network developed dementia.

Predicting Alzheimer's Disease

If you're worried about Alzheimer's disease, a diagnostic technique on the horizon may give years of advanced warning and thus more opportunity for treatment.

This is news, since the only absolute way of confirming Alzheimer's disease is by autopsying a brain (after death, of course) and finding it gummed up with plaques made up of the sticky beta-amyloid protein, along with other signs of damage. In life, a diagnosis is made through detailed neurological and neuropsychological examinations that rule out other possible diagnoses, a lengthy process that can delay treatment.

Ongoing studies at Uppsala University in Sweden have shown that a chemical agent dubbed Pittsburgh compound-B (PIB) is a highly accurate marker of plaque buildup. The amount of PIB in the brain could predict whether those with mild cognitive impairment will develop Alzheimer's disease—and when that decline will likely start.

PIB works by selectively binding to amyloid in the living brain, so a brain scan can accurately indicate the amount of protein deposit. The hope is that this technique could give Alzheimer's sufferers and their families several years of advance warning. Even more promising, experts say, is the window of opportunity for treatment. Many potential drugs for Alzheimer's disease target amyloid plaque. PIB could be a powerful tool for studying these drugs in people with mild cognitive impairment. However, in a more recent University of Pittsburgh School of Medicine study, PIB also showed up in the brains of healthy people with no signs of cognitive problems. Researchers say they aren't sure yet what that means; the studies are ongoing.

How Forgetting Is Good for the Brain

John? James? Julian? The next time someone's name stays frustratingly on the tip of your tongue, don't feel bad: your brain is just doing its job. Forgetting not only helps the brain conserve energy, it also improves our short-term memory and recall of important details, studies show.

Stanford University scientists asked students to study 240 word pairs and memorize only a small part of the list, asking them to

---

GOT DEGREES? EDUCATION DELAYS DEMENTIA, BUT NOT FOR LONG

Those years of college education may pay off in brain health—or not. People with more years of formal education tend to be diagnosed with dementia later in life, but once it starts, dementia gallops through the educated brain much faster than it does in those with less school learning, report researchers from Albert Einstein College of Medicine of Yeshiva University in New York.

A study of educated people—those with three years to more than sixteen years of formal education—found that for every additional year of schooling, memory declined 4 percent more quickly after the onset of dementia. Researchers don't know why, but they speculate that educated people could unconsciously compensate for their brain's age changes: they might actually have dementia early on but are able to hide it. By the time dementia overwhelms the brain and is diagnosed, the degeneration is actually at a later stage than in most early-stage diagnosis, and so the decline seems more rapid.

Researchers are also taking another look at the numerous studies that show challenging the brain with mental activities may delay dementia. They're wondering if such brain challenges truly protect the mind or if people who engage in them are simply better educated or smarter.

---

selectively retain some pairs and mentally discard others. MRI scans then tested them to see how well they had learned all the pairs. Those who could most often recall the pairs from the target list were also the worst at remembering the rest, suggesting that they were better at unconsciously filtering out unwanted memories. The MRI scans also showed reduced activity in the prefrontal cortex, an area associated with detecting and resolving memory conflicts. The findings suggest that memory suppression helps to conserve energy and improve efficiency—and some research indicates that efficient brains think faster.

A second study reveals that working memory (a form of short-term memory that both passively stores and actively manipulates information) benefits from an inhibition of long-term memory. Researchers investigating mice used techniques to stop the formation of new neurons in the hippocampus, which is important for long-term memory. These mice performed maze-related working-memory tasks better than normal mice did, suggesting "that by impairing one form of memory, long-term memory, it is actually possible to improve another form," says Gaël Malleret, a neuroscientist at Columbia University and coauthor of the study.

So if you accidentally call Julian "John," take heart: your brain probably just chose to dump Julian's name in favor of a more crucial fact. Such as where you left your keys.

Asleep at the Wheel–Almost? It Could Be Narcolepsy

There you are, in the middle of a conversation in the middle of the day, when suddenly your brain has put you to sleep. You may be out for a few seconds or a few minutes, and it can happen several times a day. It's narcolepsy, a sleep disorder that causes unexpected bouts of sudden sleeping and afflicts one in two thousand Americans and possibly many more. It's often not diagnosed for a decade or more, or until something goes wrong.

Most people slide into sleep through four stages of deepening slumber, ending with the dream stage of REM (rapid eye movement) sleep, and then start the cycle all over again (see "11:00 P.M."). People with narcolepsy sidestep these stages and drop almost immediately into a form of REM sleep called sleep onset rapid eye movement period. They spend much less time in refreshing deep sleep and a lot more time in REM than the rest of us and thus dream a lot more, which could explain some of that daytime fatigue.

Research shows that 90 percent of people with narcolepsy have a shortage of hypocretin, a tiny brain molecule produced in the hypothalamus, and the cells that produce it. Replacing some of those missing molecules could help, but scientists haven't discovered how to go about it yet. In the meantime, many narcopleptics take amphetamine-like stimulants to combat daytime drowsiness.

Triple espresso anyone?

1:54 P.M. Just Time for a Six-Minute Power Nap

You may be yearning for a little nap by now. If you're on the job, the boss is not likely to approve. Nevertheless, sleep researchers say you should be encouraged to grab a siesta.

Mountains of evidence show that sleep enhances memory and that short sleeps are the norm in animals, infants, and the elderly. In fact, with even a teeny-weeny six-minute nap, you stand to gain in improved short-term memory.

Olaf Lahl of the University of Düsseldorf and his colleagues struck a blow for power napping by showing that falling asleep for only six minutes is enough to significantly enhance memory. This is the shortest period of sleep found to affect mental functioning. It suggests that something happens at the point of losing consciousness that solidifies memories.

Study participants reported to the university's sleep lab at 1:00 P.M. and were given two minutes to memorize a list of thirty words and tested on their recall an hour later. In that interim, they either stayed awake, took a six-minute nap, or took a longer snooze averaging thirty-five minutes. Those on no sleep recalled an average of just under seven words. A longer nap, which included some time in deeper sleep, boosted recall to more than nine words. But even the shortest nap raised performance to more than eight words.

Some other sleep research skeptics don't think it was the nap. They think it more likely sleepiness was impairing memory than that a short nap enhanced it, and they say that in such a short time, it's hard to tell if you're even asleep.

Sounds like you need to do your own research, starting right now. . . .

Bored Bored Bored

Can't Get No Satisfaction? Maybe It's ADHD

That power nap didn't seem to help, or maybe you're among those who can't nap. Whatever. A tetchy restlessness has set in, and you can barely stand it. You just can't concentrate on the task at hand, no matter what it is. With your mind flitting everywhere and aimlessly, you get up and down from your desk, stop and start a half-dozen projects, tap your foot, drum your fingers, get coffee, get a soda, work the Internet and your e-mail obsessively.

You are bored bored bored.

Or maybe not. Maybe you've got a touch of ADHD, the attention deficit hyperactivity disorder that makes it difficult to focus, control impulses, or even sit still.

The Centers for Disease Control and Prevention estimates more than 4.4 million school-age children have been diagnosed with ADHD by a healthcare professional. Some outgrow it, but up to 80 percent still have some degree of it as adults. You could be interpreting this as boredom, since boredom is linked to problems with attention, and it's hard to be interested in something when you can't concentrate on it. Men are generally more bored than women, and more males are diagnosed with ADHD than females.

There's evidence that several genes play a role in ADHD, along with brain abnormalities and some dopamine transmission problems.

Researchers find children with ADHD have, on average, differences in the brain areas responsible for planning, impulse control, and movement. Areas such as the frontal lobe, cerebellum, and parietal and temporal lobes are smaller than in non-ADHD kids of a similar age.

They also have lower levels of dopamine, the neurotransmitter that strengthens connections between the brain's reward center and actions. When dopamine levels are low, the action-reward connection is skewed: the brain gets a much reduced reward signal, or gets it at the wrong time, or it has no effect. (See "Noon.")

RISKY BUSINESS: ARE YOU DRIVEN TO EXTREMES?

If by now your itch to do something just has to be scratched and it's prompting you to do something risky, you might have the novelty-seeking gene.

In people with the risk variant of the DRD4 gene, the neurochemical high is more likely to overrule common sense, much like the urge for cocaine hits an addict. And it takes ever more extreme risk to get the dopamine rush they crave.

In your case, you may not be driven to bungee jumping or armed robbery, but the urge for a dopamine rush could tempt you to take other risks that are dangerous to your health, your relationships, or your job. You could succumb to that urge to speed on the freeway, sneak a sex romp with someone else's spouse, or blow off the workday afternoon in a bar—all actions known to have potentially very bad outcomes.

Researchers are still collecting evidence about the effects of the DRD4 variant on personality: they find it might also be connected with sex addiction.

Brain damage can have a similar effect. Both ADHD-like behavior and risky business are connected to damage to the frontal cortex. People with these brain injuries have trouble paying attention and are prone to a number of emotional and cognitive quirks, including extreme increases in sensation seeking or risk taking.

Among the genes scientists have identified connected with ADHD is a variant of one of the dopamine receptor genes called D4, or DRD4. People who have this gene need to go to risky extremes to get a rush. These are the people you find bungee jumping and extreme skiing. They score high on a test of novelty seeking and tend to be relatively impulsive, exploratory, fickle, excitable, quick-tempered, and extravagant. Hence, it's been dubbed "the novelty-seeking gene."

A small study of ADHD children suggests the DRD4 gene might influence attention by affecting the thickness of the brain in certain places. Researchers found that those who had both ADHD and the risk variant of the gene had unusually thin tissue in two regions of the brain that govern attention. The brain tissue in these regions was somewhat thicker in children who had either the gene variant or ADHD and was thickest in children who had neither of these.

ADHD and Risk Taking Could Be Good—Sometimes

Evolution tends to knock off genetic characteristics that aren't beneficial. Under the right circumstances, ADHD and risk taking might have offered advantages in preindustrialized society, and they still could today. While kids with ADHD face difficulties in school and on the playground, ADHD qualities such as an exploratory nature and high-octane energy might be advantageous in an adult. Of course, it also helps to select occupations and lifestyles that benefit from these qualities.

When researchers recently studied two groups from the same African tribe, they found that males with the ADHD-related genes who lived a traditional nomadic lifestyle had an advantage in fitness. Dan Eisenberg, an anthropologist at Northwestern University, collected body mass index and height data on Kenyan adult males. In the nomadic group, he found that those with ADHD-related genes were better nourished than those without the gene. But those in the group who had settled down were less fit. In the same way, risk taking probably conferred an evolutionary advantage. It could have helped early humans find food and mates, and successful risk takers passed on their genes.

MAYBE WE'RE BORN WITH A WANDERING BRAIN

Don't worry if your mind is only sometimes hard to focus. According to a Harvard Medical School study, we have a network of brain regions dedicated to meandering thoughts that turns off and on, depending on how focused we need to be to complete different tasks.

Previous studies have shown that this "default" network, which is composed of at least seven separate brain regions, kicks in anytime we are at rest—say, passively taking in a TV show or a sunset. But the function of letting our gray matter go gallivanting has been unclear.

More recent studies have found that dull or unchallenging tasks switch on the default network as well. Malia F. Mason of Harvard Medical School and her colleagues scanned the brains of several subjects while their memory of short sequences of letters was being evaluated. When tested on a familiar set of letters that the subjects had been trained on for days—boring!—their daydreaming networks switched into overdrive. But when they had to focus on sorting out new combinations of letters, the networks fell quiet. This pattern matched each person's own reports of when his or her mind wandered from the tasks.

At this evolutionary point, humans have the cerebral cortex power to put the brakes on truly dangerous pleasures—sometimes. But some of us just can't avoid trouble. We can't control our impulsiveness or our urge for danger. That might make us better nomads than villagers.

Wired and Hooked: Addicted to Technology

You can't stop checking your e-mail or your cell phone, texting messages while in a meeting, talking on the phone to someone else or (egads!) while driving. Or you may pop up a video game, Facebook, or Twitter to help control your fidgets.

For a growing number of people, the hooked-up life they lead online may seem more important, more immediate, and more intense than the life they lead face-to-face. But in spite of the overwhelming impact of cell phones and the Internet on daily life just about everywhere anyone can get a signal, there's been little research on how intensive time online affects the brain.

Some studies have found a significant association between Internet addiction and the symptoms of ADHD. They have also found that ADHD-like symptoms all but disappear when ADHD kids interact with a computer: the kids might actually be using Web surfing and video games to help control their ADHD symptoms. Video games in particular offer escape and distraction: players quickly learn that they feel better when playing, and so a kind of reinforcement loop develops. They self-medicate with electronics.

Maintaining control over media habits is a challenge. Like many other addictions, Internet and cell phone addiction seems more prevalent among those of us vulnerable to addiction in general. Indeed, Internet addiction has been proposed (not completely facetiously) as a new clinical disorder. There is a Center for Internet Addiction Recovery, which has a Web site (http://www.netaddiction.com/)—and not a trace of irony about the fact that it is using the medium of addiction to supposedly treat the addiction.

3 *p.m.*

Your Pain Is Mainly in the Brain

Oh, your aching back! Maybe it's from sitting all day in an unyielding office chair, or from pulling weeds, tossing hay bales, or trundling toddlers. Come to think of it, your knees are screaming too, that back molar is throbbing, and your head feels as if it's in a vise. You are in pain.

And, yes, it *is* all in your head. Sure, it's your back/knee/tooth/temples that are screaming. But the perception of pain is in the brain. And right now, that pain is keeping you from thinking about anything else.

The pain message gets sent to the brain via specialized neurons called nociceptors, which sit outside the central nervous system. Their job is to detect potentially harmful happenings to your body, such as extremes of temperature, unusual pressure, or chemicals released in response to an injury or inflammation.

Nociceptors have two arms: a sensation-detecting branch that projects outward to the periphery of your body and a second branch that extends into the spinal cord. When these detect trouble, they telegraph an impulse up the line to an area of the spinal cord called the dorsal horn, which relays the alarm message to your brain, which is when we cry, "Ouch!"

Some pain is good. Acute pain is an alarm in your brain telling you something is wrong in your body—that toe you stubbed is bleeding or maybe broken. Better stop whatever you're doing, and see to it. Without that alert, we wouldn't know when we've damaged something;

untreated injuries can lead to serious health issues. And when you fix the injury, the pain gradually goes away.

How Pain Hurts Your Brain

When pain never goes away, it becomes chronic—an alarm that never gets turned off—and it can literally rewire you. It can shrink parts of your brain and interfere with your ability to make good decisions. It surely makes your life miserable.

Unrelenting pain is, in fact, a disease in itself. Research shows that over time, chronic pain alters your nervous system and can lead to more pain: it can make structural changes in your nerve cells that make them supersensitive, or cause them to fire off pain signals when nothing is happening, or change the pain transmission pathways in your central nervous system.

You can actually see striking differences in a brain in pain. An imaging study showed greater-than-normal brain atrophy in gray matter density in the prefrontal cortex and in overall brain volume in people with chronic back pain, concluded A. Vania Apkarian, a bioelectrical engineer and physiologist at Northwestern University.

And if you have chronic pain, skip the poker table. The same researcher found that pain affects emotional decision making. He asked twenty-six people who had suffered lower back pain for more than one year and twenty-nine normal volunteers to play a gambling card game to study decision making in risky, emotionally laden situations. Those with chronic pain made 40 percent fewer good choices compared with those made by nonsufferers. What's more, the amount of suffering correlated with how badly they played.

Mind Under Matter, Mind over Brain

Pain wins in the battle for your brain's attention, no doubt. Everyone knows that it's impossible to concentrate when pain is shrieking your name. Now neuroscientists have proved it.

Researchers at the University Medical Center Hamburg-Eppendorf in Germany have identified a region of the brain that processes both working memory and pain, and it seems to give preference to pain.

YOUR BRAIN ITSELF HAS NO PAIN

Curiously, the outside of your brain doesn't feel a thing. Surgeons can, and do, touch the outer surface of brains. That's because perception of any stimulus, including pain, depends on sensory neurons and your brain and other internal organs don't have very many of these. In fact, internal organs house only about 2 to 5 percent of all sensory neurons in the body.

Because of this, we can keep close touch (literally) with the world around us but have limited conscious awareness of our innards—possibly because most threats arise externally. Nociceptors do exist near your brain: they're in its blood vessels and in the meninges, the thin membranes that wrap around and protect the brain and spinal cord. One of the sources of migraine headache pain may arise from the nociceptors in the meninges.

Our other internal body parts also tend to have nociceptors in the surrounding tissue, alerting us if they are stretched or squeezed. Interestingly, when those few nociceptors inside an organ are stimulated, the pain is "referred" to regions on the surface of the body. This phenomenon explains why the pain that may accompany a stroke is commonly felt in muscles and joints, particularly in the shoulder region. Although the stroke is damaging the brain, the brain doesn't sense the pain in itself.

Using functional magnetic resonance imaging (fMRI) scans, the researchers found that applying pain to volunteers' hands as they worked on a visual task increased activity in brain areas involved in pain processing while decreasing activity in areas that were working on the assigned task.

Ulrike Bingel, who led the study, says the work might have implications for pain management. When doctors decide whether to prescribe strong painkillers such as opiates, they consider the thought-blurring side effects, but they don't always consider that the pain itself can interfere with mental function.

The right distraction, however, can triumph over pain. Today's virtual reality games might be made for this. They immerse users in a three-dimensional computer-generated world uniquely suited to distracting people from their pain. Burn patients undergoing wound care report that their pain drops dramatically when they're engaged in virtual reality programs, and fMRIs back that up, showing a reduction in pain-related activity in the brain.

And the placebo effect works in some cases. People who expected to get relief may actually produce it by inducing chemical changes in the brain, a University of Michigan at Ann Arbor study found. Researchers gave test subjects a slow, long, harmless injection of a pain-inducing salt solution into the jaw while they scanned brains with positron emission tomography (PET), asking subjects to rate pain. Then the researchers said—falsely—that they had just added pain-relieving serum into the solution and asked again for pain ranking. The PET scans found particular regions of the brain produced painkilling endorphins in people who said they felt less uncomfortable, right after the placebo was promised.

Is Hypnosis Real?

Yes, hypnosis is real, and it may help with pain control, but many popular ideas about it are not. In fact, during hypnosis, individuals are not under control of the hypnotist, they usually remember everything that happens when hypnotized, and memories they "recall" under hypnotism aren't infallibly true.

Hypnosis is sustained, focused attention coupled with suggestions for changes in experience, perception, emotion, thought, or behavior. But not everyone can be hypnotized. Certain people are simply more susceptible to it than others. The degree to which a person can be hypnotized and influenced depends on his or her natural ability to experience hypnosis rather than on the "power" of the hypnotist or any particular technique.

Science isn't sure how hypnosis works, but evidence indicates that hypnotic suggestions affect specific parts of the brain and can modify

THE UNITED STATES IS A COUNTRY IN PAIN

We are a hurting nation, according to a survey of 3,982 Americans. In an attempt to understand daily aches, Alan B. Krueger of Princeton University and Arthur A. Stone of Stony Brook University in New York asked respondents to rate their pain on a scale of 0 (none) to 6 (very strong) at three random intervals during the waking hours of every day. The study reveals a "pain gap," with poorer, less educated people suffering more than wealthier, more educated individuals. Not surprisingly, pain affects life satisfaction. Here are the statistics:

Percentage of Americans in pain at any given time: 28

Percentage of those in pain who:
- Earn less than $30,000: 34.2
- Earn more than $100,000: 22.9
- Did not finish high school: 33
- Got a college degree: 20.2
- Are not satisfied with life: 53.9
  - Average pain rating: 2.26
- Are very satisfied with life: 22.4
  - Average pain rating: 0.66

Amount spent annually on:
- Nonprescription painkillers: $2.6 billion
- Outpatient prescription painkillers: $13.8 billion

Productivity lost annually because of pain: $60 billion

the way the brain processes information. Researchers have used hypnosis to study one kind of forgetting: functional amnesia, a sudden memory loss connected with psychological trauma rather than damage or disease.

A Window into Traumatic Forgetting

Hypnotists can produce a reversible posthypnotic amnesia (PHA) in some susceptible people: when hypnotized, they're told to forget something until they get a "cancellation" cue such as the phrase, "Now you can remember everything," and the memories come flooding back.

This temporary inability to retrieve selective information that is safely stored in the memory has intrigued researchers. In what has been called a groundbreaking study, Avi Mendelsohn and colleagues at the Weizmann Institute in Israel identified specific brain activity patterns in this type of hypnosis.

They chose two groups of people, one group that was suggestible to PHA and one that was not. They showed them a forty-five-minute movie, hypnotized them while they lay in an fMRI scanner, and gave them a forgetting suggestion. Later, when the PHA group was tested while being imaged with fMRI, researchers found, not surprisingly, that the group had trouble remembering the movie but not the context in which they saw it. What was surprising is what happened in their brains. In contrast to the non-PHA people, the PHA group showed little or no activity in the visual areas (occipital lobe) or verbal area (temporal lobe) but more activity in the prefrontal cortex, which is responsible for regulating other brain areas.

This suggests that the brain moved quickly to suppress some memories in amnesia and gives insight into the brain processes in people with traumatic memory loss. But scientists still don't know how the brain decides what to suppress or exactly how it works.

They do know that hypnosis can be a valuable tool for pain control for some people. When used responsibly by medical professionals as one part of a treatment plan, hypnosis can help with some emotional and medical problems. For example, if you hear a hypnotic suggestion

STICKING POINT: ACUPUNCTURE CHANGES YOUR BRAIN

Sometimes you can needle your pain away. The ancient oriental therapy of acupuncture is increasingly suggested for pain relief. It supposedly stimulates the invisible "energy channels" in your body through specific placement of hair-fine needles. Science hasn't found these energy channels, but acupuncture does have an effect on some people.

Studies by scientists at the China Academy for Traditional Chinese Medicine in Beijing and at Harvard Medical School used functional magnetic resonance imaging (fMRI) to see whether needles inserted in the hand changed brain activity. They found decreased activity in the hippocampus, hypothalamus, and other parts of the limbic system, which is known to be involved in feeling pain, and changes in the activity of the somatosensory cortex, a brain region involved in processing pain as well as other sensory input.

So far, they don't know why. It could be that needles prompt the release of endorphins. Or it could be that people—and brains—who get acupuncture react to the focused one-on-one attention of therapy.

that you will not feel pain, certain areas of the brain may still register that painful stimulus but the brain's normal "emotional" reaction is muted. Hypnosis can also help some people who suffer from pain or debilitating anxiety or wish to curb addictions or lose weight. But hypnosis is almost never a stand-alone treatment and is not a foolproof way to cure unhealthy habits.

4 p.m.

Exercise Your Brain

The end of the workday is in sight, and your brain is relieved. So is your mind, which has been doing heavy lifting, and your body, with all of its aches and pains.

So this is the perfect time to exercise. Really.

Okay, late afternoon may not be the most convenient time in your schedule, but a number of researchers are saying it's the best time for your body. Studies find that body temperature tends to be at its highest in late afternoon, making muscles more supple and lowering the risk of injury. And exercise at any time is excellent for your brain.

Exercise Grows Neurons and Improves Memory

If you ever needed another reason to hit the gym, this could be the kicker: new research suggests that working out may improve memory by ramping up the creation of new brain cells.

Previous research has shown that exercise spurs neuron formation in mice, so scientists at Columbia University and the Salk Institute for Biological Studies in San Diego wanted to know whether this neuro-genesis (neuron growth) also occurs in humans. They knew that adult brains spawn new neurons in only two locations. Fortunately, one of them is the dentate gyrus, a region in the hippocampus linked to age-related memory decline. The researchers theorized that if exercise triggers neurogenesis in the human dentate gyrus, then exercising could improve memory and help prevent its loss in old age.

Neurogenesis is difficult to study, however, because the only way to find direct evidence for newborn neurons is in an autopsy. To look for neurogenesis in living people, the scientists needed to find a proxy—a marker indicating neuron formation that could be detected without cutting into a brain. They compared MRI scans of mice that had been working out regularly for two weeks with scans of sedentary mice and found that exercise increased blood flow in the dentate gyrus. Postmortem mouse exams confirmed this was a sign of the birth of new brain cells.

The scientists then compared magnetic resonance imaging scans of people who exercised regularly with those of couch potatoes. Just as in the mice, the exercisers had more blood flowing in their dentate gyrus, suggesting that neurogenesis was also occurring there. Finally, the scientists gave tests to see if exercise actually improved memory. They found that the more physically fit the people were, the better they performed on word memory tasks. In the words of one researcher, "Exercise is brain food."

WHATEVER WORKS—JUST WORK OUT

The time for exercise isn't written in stone. Although researchers are now touting late afternoon, some people feel that if they don't hit the gym first thing in the morning, they won't do it at all. Others prefer a lunchtime break, especially if there's a gym at the workplace. Right after work is good for some.

But don't let obsessing about the optimal time of day stop you. A look at the studies that show exercise builds new neurons should be enough to get your brain interested: it's self-preservation. Experiment with different times of day to see what suits your clock best. The only time-connected rule is not to exercise immediately following a meal. Wait ninety minutes after a heavy meal.

Now all you have to do is get your mind to get your brain and body to the gym.

Why We Get Food Cravings

Sometimes it's a yen for salsa and chips, a bowl of ice cream, or, during pregnancy, salsa, chips, *and* ice cream. Right about now, it's for a double-chocolate cookie. You can say your body is craving that cookie.

While hankerings for certain foods don't seem to have anything to do with obvious nutrient lacks, other biology may be at work. Imaging data from functional magnetic resonance imaging (fMRI) studies suggest that pining for a certain food activates a bunch of brain areas, including components of the amygdala, anterior cingulate, orbital frontal cortex, insula, hippocampus, caudate, and dorsolateral prefrontal cortex. Indeed, a network of neural regions may be involved, including with those of emotion and memory, as well as the chemosensory centers.

Take that urge for chocolate. Something in chocolate may influence your feelings of satiation or your longing for the treat by affecting mood-influencing chemicals in your brain, including serotonin and tryptophan. Other foods contain these compounds at higher concentrations, but there's no contest: they aren't as appealing as chocolate.

Some investigators suggest simple carbohydrate content may increase a food's appeal for you. More support for a nutrition-neurological connection comes from research that shows that naloxone, which blocks opiate receptors in the brain, appears to inhibit the appeal of sweet, high-fat foods such as chocolate.

Research on hunger-control mechanisms in the gastrointestinal tract has identified an entire spectrum of gut neuropeptides with elaborate central nervous system feedback and influence on satiety. (See "Noon.")

And then there are some studies that suggest that chocolate craving, especially among women, could partly be about a sense of deprivation or a reaction to stress, perimenstrual hormonal changes, and other chemistry. But, researchers concede, culture has an influence as well. And don't forget the impact of remembered pleasure.

So pass the chocolate cookies.

The Most Dangerous Time for Teens

If you're a teen (or have one), the after school hours could be your most dangerous time of day. The peak time for teens to commit violence or to be a victim of it is on school days between 2:00 P.M. 6:00 P.M., according to data from the Office of Juvenile Justice and Delinquency Prevention. On nonschool days, juvenile violence increases through the afternoon and early evening hours, peaking between 7:00 P.M. and 9:00 P.M.

Although the records don't speculate on the reasons, these afterschool hours are the least supervised. Without supervision, teens may experiment with sex, alcohol, drugs, or gang activity. And if you've thought teens are drawn to risky business because the teen brain is still a work in process, many experts agree. In fact, that's what the National Institute of Mental Health calls it.

The Teen Brain Is Still Changing

No doubt, its tough to be a teen (and to live with one). It can be the best of times, the worst of times—to which some of you will grunt, "There are NO good times when you live with teens."

But if parental units (and sundry related familial types) are suffering, pity the poor teen. This is a time of enormous change, and not just in the body but in the brain as well. The brain goes through its most drastic restructuring in the teen years than at any other time between birth and death (ruling out major injury).

Studies show that the developing human brain has an overproduction and then pruning of gray matter (neurons) in the womb and in the first two years after birth. Magnetic resonance imaging shows a similar surge in the teen years. Some researchers say that the prefrontal cortex in the teen brain is still developing, which contributes to all that turmoil, bad decisions, and risky business.

There are some differences between the teen and adult brains—at least some teen brains. A small Australian study that imaged the brains of teens arguing with parents (sound familiar?) found a link between brain structure and aggression. Teens of either gender who had a larger amygdala stayed angry longer, as did boys with a smaller left anterior cingulate cortex (a prefrontal area connected with reason, among other activities). They note that the research needs follow-up, as teen years are a period of rapid brain development and change.

Other experts disagree. They suggest it's the "artificial extension of childhood" in contemporary Western cultures that leads to many teen troubles. In other societies, children are expected to assume many adult responsibilities as they reach their teens, and they do, as teens have done in times past. Many preindustrial societies don't even have a word or concept for adolescence.

But Don't Forget Hormones

There's little doubt that surging hormones affect behavior, including teen behavior. As if to prove an innate contrariness in teens, a hormone that usually reduces anxiety and calms brain activity in adults and children has the opposite effect on adolescents. The chemical THP (allopregnanolone) excites the teen brain, increases anxiety and panic, and may lead to teen suicide, according to investigators at the State University of New York Downstate Medical Center who looked at teen depression and mental illness.

THP is a steroid created in the body when progesterone, a sex hormone, is metabolized. It is usually released in the brain in response to stress and quiets the neural system within thirty minutes by binding to so-called gamma-aminobutyric acid receptors on the surfaces of neurons. But it has the reverse effect in teens. Research on female mice (because girls are twice as likely as boys to have anxiety disorders in puberty) has yielded insights that could help with new treatments for depression and stress targeting THP.

Part 4

2
3
4

Time Out

letting go and coming home

5 p.m. to 8 p.m.

5 *p.m.*

The Dimming of the Day

The day is dimming, and so are you. As the day winds down, your spirits may be sinking, darkening with the light, especially in the early winter evenings. You may have the blahs or the blues or just feel down, low, bummed out. You are, you say, depressed.

Is It Really Depression? Or Just a Bad Patch?

Don't get upset if someone suggests your brain may not really be depressed. Certainly most of us would attribute our dulled-down feelings to depression. The term describes how we feel, and it's one of the top mental health diagnoses today. But the fact is that true chronic clinical depression is not that common.

For most of us, what we call depression is a temporary state, perhaps related to what's happening (or not) in our life right now. Or it can be seasonal (see "Maybe You're Just SAD" later in the chapter). Clinical depression, however, is a serious and chronic disease, with accordingly more serious symptoms. People with major depression don't just have the blues: they are unable to feel any pleasure or interest in anything, unable to concentrate, have dramatic weight loss or gain, and have equally dramatic extremes of either sleeping all the time or being unable to sleep. They may be consumed with self-loathing and unable to connect with anyone or anything, and they are at high risk of suicide. And these feelings don't go away.

Clocks in the Brain
Your Circadian Clock

Circadian comes from the Latin circa ("about") and diem ("a day"). The daily cycles of light and dark influence many of our physiological activities and rhythms. These are determined in part by your master body clock, a bundle of neurons called the suprachiasmatic nucleus (SCN). This tiny master clock—no bigger than a grain of rice and buried deep in your brain—helps control many daily rhythms and organ activities, including your sleep/wake cycle. During daylight, changes in light are detected by ganglion cells in the retina in your eyes and passed along to the SCN. The SCN fires off signals (red arrow) that suppress pineal gland secretion of melatonin, the "sleep hormone."

After dark, however, the SCN takes off the brake, allowing the paraventricular nucleus to send a "secrete melatonin" signal (green arrows) through neurons in the upper spine and the neck to the pineal gland. The SCN firing rate drops, and melatonin flows into the bloodstream, helping make you drowsy.

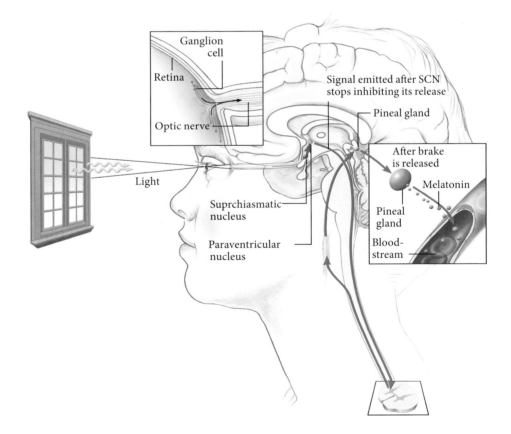

Gateway to Consciousness

Although experts are still debating consciousness, it's agreed we consciously perceive only information that is processed in the associative regions of the cerebral cortex. But many other brain regions that operate on a subconscious level also participate in the various levels of consciousness. One is the reticular activating system (RAS), a formation in the brain stem that plays a major role in keeping you alert, regulating activity and consciousness in the cerebral cortex, your thinking brain. It projects widely through the brain, taking in information from various neural pathways to tell your thinking brain when there is a new or persistent stimuli. Many of its fibers come through the thalamus, the reception room for the cerebral cortex.

Other brain sections, especially the pedunculopontine tegmental nucleus (PPT) and the locus coeruleus (blue spot), signal the presence and the importance of stimuli with neurotransmitters norepinephrine and acetylcholine, influencing focused attention and memory formation. The dorsal raphe nucleus is involved in balancing emotions and cognition with serotonin.

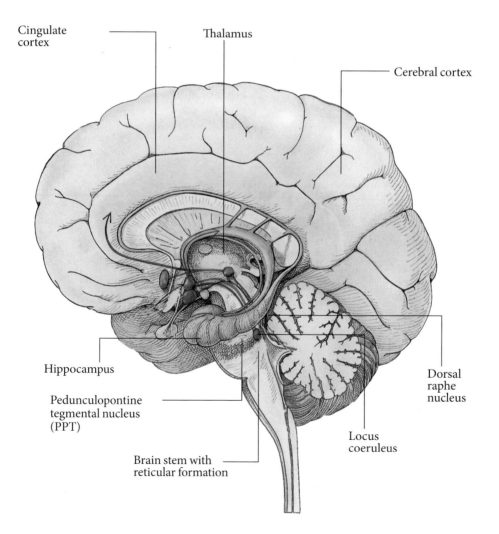

Cingulate cortex

Thalamus

Cerebral cortex

Hippocampus

Pedunculopontine tegmental nucleus (PPT)

Dorsal raphe nucleus

Locus coeruleus

Brain stem with reticular formation

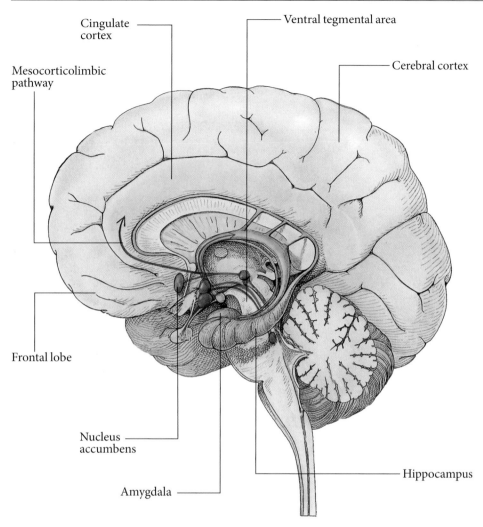

Cingulate cortex

Ventral tegmental area

Mesocorticolimbic pathway

Cerebral cortex

Frontal lobe

Nucleus accumbens

Hippocampus

Amygdala

Emotions and Memory

Our emotions are shaped by the impact of the limbic system—our emotional and primitive brain center—on the thinking brain, the cerebral cortex. The amygdala rules here: an almond-shaped nucleus at the center of the limbic system, it generates and processes unconscious emotions and experiences, especially those from our environment that are frightening or could be dangerous. It could also deal with curiosity and the will to action.

Emotions of desire, satisfaction, and contentment are related to the mesolimbic system, which contains the nucleus accumbens and the ventral tegmental area—components of the so-called reward circuit. These use dopamine to alert the rest of your brain when a positive or desirable circumstance presents itself. Memory, which is mediated by the hippocampus, is vital to consciousness. The cingulate cortex, which sits midway between the limbic system and the cerebral cortex, controls alertness and the emotional coloring of perception. It also helps to recognize and correct mistakes.

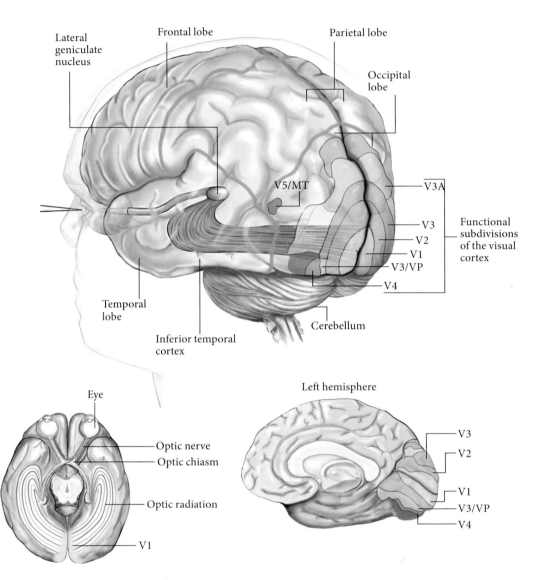

Lateral geniculate nucleus

Frontal lobe

Parietal lobe

Occipital lobe

V5/MT

V3A

V3

V2

V1

V3/VP

V4

Functional subdivisions of the visual cortex

Temporal lobe

Inferior temporal cortex

Cerebellum

Eye

Left hemisphere

Optic nerve

Optic chiasm

Optic radiation

V1

V3

V2

V1

V3/VP

V4

Structures for Seeing

Seeing begins with the eyes but travels through several parts of the brain before it comes to the primary visual cortex (see V1, V2, and so on). The optic nerves cross over partially (at the optic chasm) so that each hemisphere of the brain receives input from both eyes, which it will combine for three-dimensional vision. Information is filtered by the layers of cells in the lateral geniculate nucleus, which respond only to stimuli from one eye. Other brain parts are involved as well. The parietal and temporal lobes interpret what the brain is "seeing."

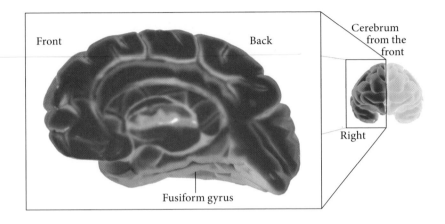

Front   Back

Cerebrum from the front

Right

Fusiform gyrus

A Cerebral Spot for Faces

Some researchers believe there is a specific spot in the brain that helps us recognize each other. It's a pea-sized spot called the fusiform face place in fusiform gyrus, a spindle-shaped area where the temporal lobe meets the occipital lobe. The fusiform gyrus is known to help process color and object recognition, while the fusiform face place is believed to be dedicated to human faces—but not all scientists agree that's its only function, or that face recognition is limited to that one tiny spot. Still, it's amazing how we recognize one another when human faces are so similar.

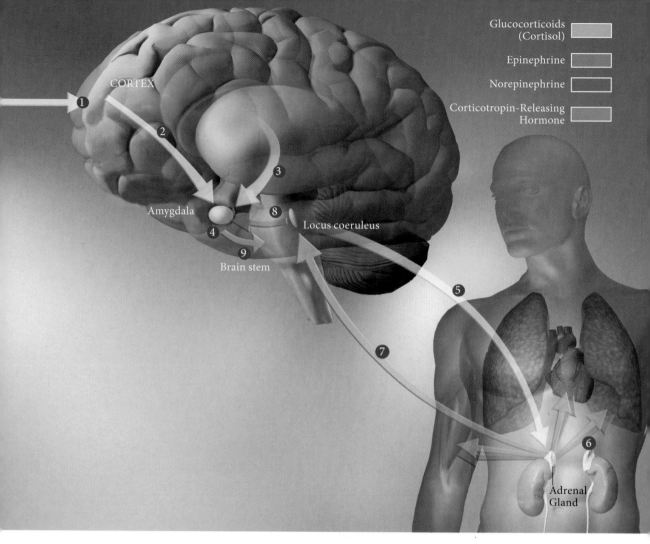

Glucocorticoids (Cortisol)

Epinephrine

Norepinephrine

Corticotropin-Releasing Hormone

CORTEX

Amygdala

Locus coeruleus

Brain stem

Adrenal Gland

The Vicious Cycle of Stress

The pathways that stress travels in your brain and body are diverse and can catch your brain in feedback loops that greatly exaggerate a response. The process—simplified here—usually begins when an actual or perceived threat activates the sensory and thinking centers in the cortex (1). The cortex sends a message to the amygdala, your internal sentry and the major mediator of the stress response (2). The amygdala might also be activated by a separate, preconscious signal (3). It responds by popping out corticotropin-releasing hormone (CRH), which stimulates the brain stem (4) to activate the sympathetic nervous system via the spinal cord (5). That prompts the adrenal glands to produce the stress hormone epinephrine and to release glucocorticoids (cortisol). These two hormones rev up muscles, heart, and lungs to prepare the body for "fight or flight" (6). If the stress becomes chronic, the cycle doesn't end: glucocorticoids induce the locus coeruleus (7) to release norepinephrine, which alerts the amygdala (8), leading to production of more CRH (9), and to an ongoing reactivation of stress.

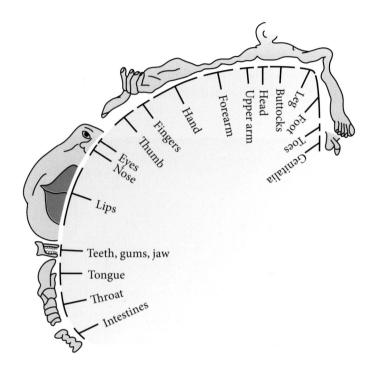

Sensory Homunculus

Your body doesn't "feel" tactile sensation equally: some areas are much more richly endowed with nerve endings. Correspondingly, your brain's primary somatosensory cortex contains a distorted "map" of the body called the sensory homunculus. This drawing shows how the areas more densely packed with sensory receptors, such as our lips, appear disproportionately large because they are more acutely sensitive.

Feeling the Pain

The pain circuit, shown here in simplified form, extends from the edges of your body and organs—the skin and other tissues outside the central nervous system—to the spinal cord and brain. When special pain-sensing nerve cells (nociceptors, in pink), perceive a harmful stimulus, they telegraph word of the trouble to nerve cells in the dorsal horn region of the spinal cord (in blue). Those cells, in turn, pass the message to your brain, where it gets interpreted as pain.

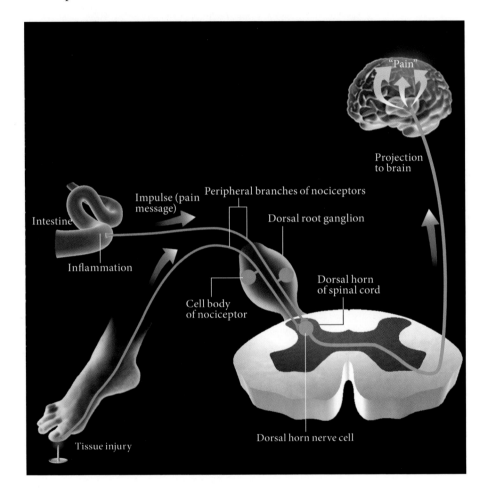

The Fear Response

When you see—or think you see—a snake in your path, your brain gets busy with a fear response. Visual stimuli go first to the thalamus, the reception and relay center for sensory input. It passes rough, almost archetypal, information to the ever-vigilant amygdala (red) which gears up for possible danger by putting the body on alert (green). It sends commands to the hypothalamus, which causes stress hormones to be released that raise blood pressure and ready the body to face the threat. Meanwhile, with a bit more time and processing, the visual cortex also receives signals from the thalamus (blue). It either confirms the danger or, if the cortex determines that the object is not a snake after all, sends a message to the amygdala to quell the fear response.

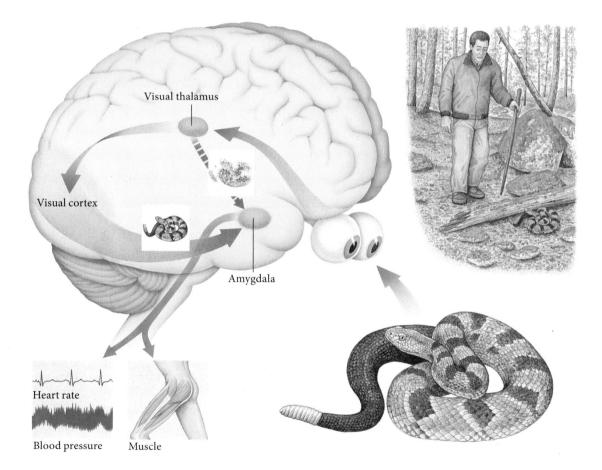

Visual thalamus

Visual cortex

Amygdala

Heart rate

Blood pressure   Muscle

Singing in the Brain

Listening to music lights up your brain, including areas usually involved in other kinds of thinking. Your personal visual, tactile, and emotional experiences all affect where your brain processes music.

We hear incoming sounds, or air pressure waves, as they are converted by the external and middle ear into fluid waves in the inner ear. A tiny bone, the stapes, pushes into the cochlea, creating varying pressure on the fluid inside. Vibrations in the membrane of the cochlea then cause inner hair cells—the sensory receptors—to generate electrical signals to the auditory nerve, which transmits them to the brain. These individual inner hair cells are tuned to different vibration frequencies.

The brain processes music within the overall auditory cortex: the primary auditory cortex receives inputs from the ear and lower auditory system via the thalamus, which is involved in the early perception of musical sound such as pitch (a tone's frequency) and contour (the pattern of changes in pitch), which is the basis for melody.

Experience hearing music "retunes" the primary auditory cortex so that more cells become more responsive to important sounds and musical tones.

This learning-induced retuning in turn affects further processing in areas such as the secondary auditory cortical fields and the so-called auditory association regions, which are thought to process more complex music patterns of harmony, melody, and rhythm.

And when you are playing an instrument, it is yet again different: other areas activate, including the motor cortex and cerebellum, which are key to the planning and performance of specific, precisely timed movements.

How and where music is processed depends not just on your hearing but on who is listening: their knowledge of music, their experience as a musician, and whether they are focusing on separate tones and rhythms or the entire melody.

When the brain of an amateur musician processes simple rhythmic relations in a tune, such as changes in length between certain tones, that brain uses the premotor regions and sections of the parietal lobe in the left hemisphere. The cerebellum (involved in movement control) also participates. If the music is more complex, then the frontal lobe in the right hemisphere chips in. But experienced musicians generally process rhythms in the frontal and temporal lobes of the right hemisphere.

Processing pitch and melody is also different between amateur and experienced musicians. The inexperienced musician activates the right posterior frontal lobe and right upper temporal lobe when comparing different pitches. But the pros show increased activity in the left hemisphere when differentiating among pitches or chords.

And when the listener focuses on whole melodies (rather than individual tones or chords), entirely different brain parts react. Activity is concentrated in the right hemisphere, in the primary and secondary auditory cortices, and the auditory associative regions in the upper temporal lobe.

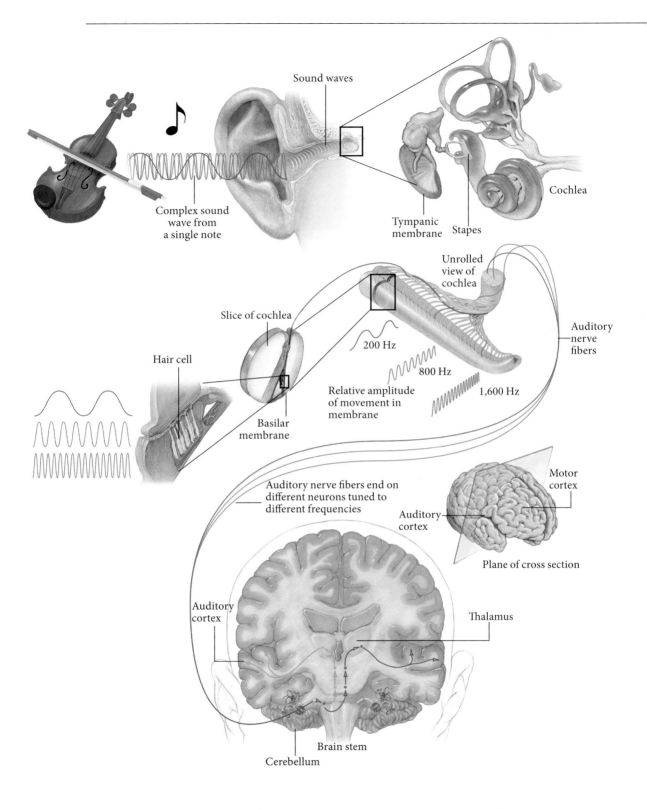

Sound waves

Cochlea

Complex sound
wave from
a single note

Tympanic
membrane

Stapes

Unrolled
view of
cochlea

Slice of cochlea

Auditory
nerve
fibers

Hair cell

200 Hz

800 Hz

1,600 Hz

Basilar
membrane

Relative amplitude
of movement in
membrane

Auditory nerve fibers end on
different neurons tuned to
different frequencies

Motor
cortex

Auditory
cortex

Auditory
cortex

Plane of cross section

Thalamus

Brain stem

Cerebellum

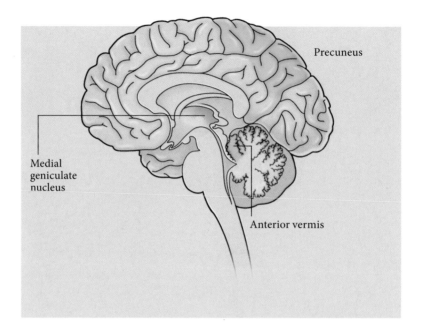

Precuneus

Medial geniculate nucleus

Anterior vermis

Mental Choreography

Dancing involves brain regions that go beyond just making voluntary movements.

Anterior vermis
This part of the cerebellum seems to act like a metronome, taking data from the spinal cord and helping synchronize dance steps to music.

Medial genticulation nucleus
This step along the lower auditory pathway seems to help set the brain's metronome and connects directly to the cerebellum without communicating with the higher auditory areas in the cortex. It underlies that tendency to unconsciously tap our toes or sway to music.

Precuneus
The precuneus has a sensory-based "map" of your body. It helps plot a dancer's path from a body-centered perspective.

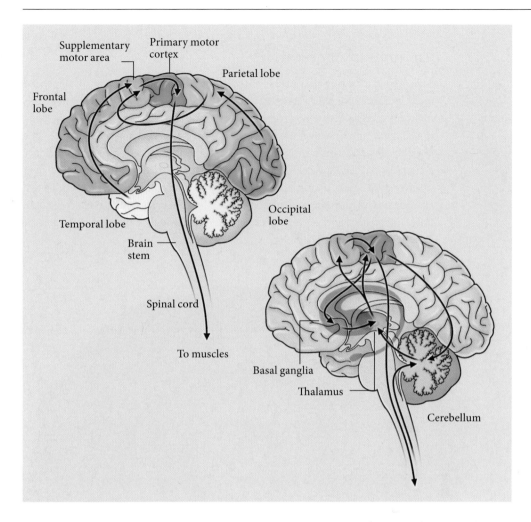

The Brain's Moving Parts

It takes a multitude of brain parts to move your body when and how you want to. Here's the simple version.

Motion planning (left) for voluntary movement occurs in the frontal lobe, where the premotor cortex on the outer surface (not visible here) and the supplementary motor area evaluate signals (arrows) from elsewhere in the brain that retrieve memories of past actions and tell where your body is in space. These two areas then communicate with the primary motor cortex, which decides what needs to happen—which muscles to contract and by how much—and sends these instructions down through the spinal cord to the muscles.

Fine tuning (right) occurs, in part, as the muscles return signals back to the brain. The cerebellum uses the feedback from the muscles to help maintain balance and refine movements. In addition, the basal ganglia collect sensory information from cortical regions and convey it through the thalamus to motor areas of the cortex.

Anatomy of Aggression

Scientists are finding that problems with the prefrontal cortex of some people make it harder for them to exercise restraint. The areas involved in decision making, such as the orbitofrontal cortex, are believed to damp down actions in the hypothalamus and the amygdala, where fear and aggression arise. But if a defect blocks this communication, a person might not be able to moderate emotional reactions, such as anger. Damage to the hippocampus may also interfere with processing emotional information, and a malfunction of the amygdala may underlie violent behavior. These theories could explain the lack of fear, empathy, and regret characteristic of criminals who plan and commit violent acts in cold blood.

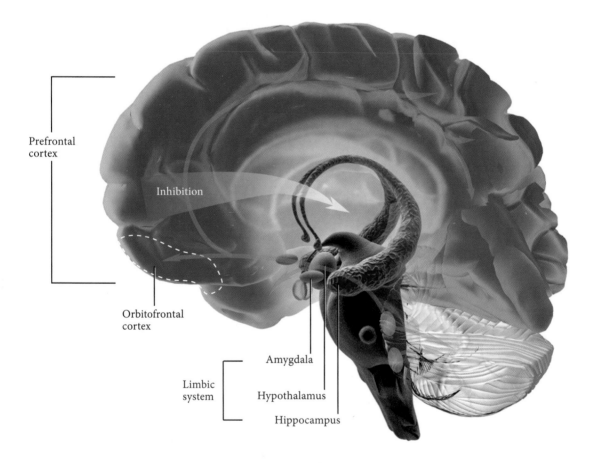

Prefrontal cortex

Inhibition

Orbitofrontal cortex

Limbic system

Amygdala

Hypothalamus

Hippocampus

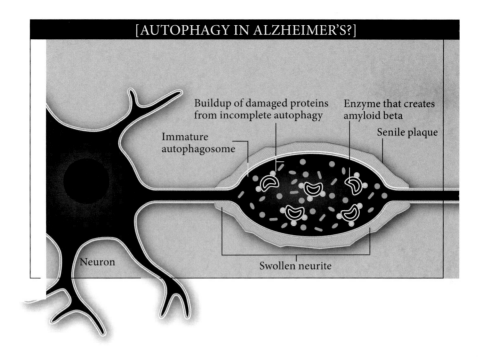

[AUTOPHAGY IN ALZHEIMER'S?]

When the Cleaning Stops

Your brain is constantly cleaning house to remove damaged proteins and other worn-out bits that clog up your neurons and contribute to swelling in the neurites that project from brain cells. But in an aging brain, the autophagosomes that gobble up neural garbage may not completely develop, and instead they become part of the trash. Enzymes (yellow) that create protein fragments called amyloid beta seem to concentrate on these immature autophagosomes. These fragments collect on the outside of neurons (orange) and form the senile plaque characteristic of brains with Alzheimer's disease, suggesting that bad neural housekeeping may contribute to dementia.

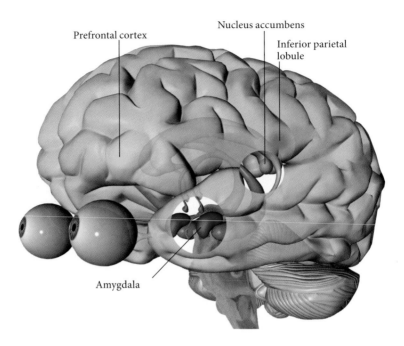

Prefrontal cortex

Nucleus accumbens

Inferior parietal lobule

Amygdala

Humor in the Brain

Appreciating a good joke involves a network of brain regions. Studies point to the prefrontal cortex (yellow) as the front row audience. It's known that damage to that area disrupts your ability to grasp and react emotionally to jokes. Some research even hints that the funnier the joke, the more active the prefrontal cortex becomes. Other studies show the amygdala (your emotional brain center) and the nucleus accumbens and other parts of your reward circuit (both in red) to be essential to appreciating humor.

And it could be that the brain area responding to humor depends on the personality of the individual. A researcher found that in extroverted people the prefrontal cortex and nearby orbiofrontal cortex light up, while for introverts, the amygdala and front part of the temporal lobes become active. This could mean pleasurable feelings (for humor, at least) originate in different brain sites for extroverts and introverts. And cheerful people may process humor in other brain areas. Those looking at Gary Larson cartoons had activity in the inferior parietal lobule (green), an area involved in resolving incongruities, and a skill essential for processing humor. Scientists speculate that activity in this area characterized someone who is easily amused and enjoys ambiguity.

This is the real thing. Brain imaging shows that depressed people have abnormalities in parts of the limbic system, parts of the prefrontal cortex, and other brain areas, as well as imbalances in neurotransmitter levels. In fact, many believe chemical imbalances are a main reason for depression.

There's a lot of evidence for the chemistry-gone-wrong theories. The antidepressant selective serotonin reuptake inhibitor drugs such as Prozac relieve depression by increasing available serotonin in the brain. Newer research has found abnormally low blood concentration levels of a protein growth factor called brain-derived neurotrophic factor (BDNF) in depressed women. When they took antidepressants, their BDNF levels returned to normal. Other research has shown that ketamine, a drug already used as a painkiller and anesthetic, relieved depressive symptoms in some people within hours, although scientists aren't sure how or why.

Searching for the Pathway to Depression

The mystery of clinical depression is that there are many causes and many treatments—and therefore plenty of theories about the psychological and physical causes. Chemistry alone can't be the cause, as up to 40 percent of people don't respond to antidepressant medications. (See "Magnetic Energy May Work When Meds Fail," page 113.)

While most researchers agree that depression is probably due to a combination of factors (including genes, environment, and individual biochemistry), they are looking for a brain pathway or abnormality to explain major clinical depression. Recent research seems to have pinpointed a spot in the hippocampus that serves as a marker for depression and might lead the way to finding a common cause. High-speed camera snapshots of rat brains found that electrical chatter in their dentate gyrus—a C-shaped region of the hippocampus—contracts in depressed rats but expands again after they are dosed with antidepressants. The hippocampus sends and receives information to and from many other brain regions, so this region could be a common pathway or intersection for brain activity in those with depression, says Karl Deisseroth, a Stanford University neuroengineer and psychiatrist.

To induce depression-like symptoms in the rats, researchers blasted static noise or other environmental annoyances at unpredictable intervals for several weeks. The chronically stressed rats placed in a tank of water swam less vigorously, indicating (apparently) their feelings of rodent hopelessness.

The team then took brain slices from "depressed" and "normal" rats, soaked them in voltage-sensitive dye, and prodded them with electrodes next to a high-speed camera trained on the hippocampus—a part of the brain known to play a role in mood and depression, as well as learning and memory. When brain cells fired, the dye was activated, showing differences in the reactions of normal and depressed rat brains.

Finding a common brain process or pathway to depression could help uncover more effective treatments, they said.

Maybe You're Just SAD

The shortened days of winter bring on the SAD-ness (seasonal affective disorder) in some of us around this time of evening. SAD, which affects many people in northern climes where light levels are lower in the winter, is connected with an increase in melatonin, a decrease in serotonin, and a mix-up in the SCN, our internal body clock.

The suprachiasmatic nucleus (SCN) signals the release of melatonin at night and shuts off the flow with morning light (see 5:00 A.M., "Waking to the World"). In people with SAD, the seasonal changes that bring longer nights and shorter days seem to confuse the SCN. It flips the switch for night mode earlier and keeps them there longer in the morning. Some have described it as being in constant jet lag.

Light deprivation can have sweeping effects. Scientists are finding it can upset other brain chemistry and kill neurons, at least in rats. When neuroscientists at the University of Pennsylvania kept rats in the dark for six weeks, the animals acted depressed and showed brain damage in the regions known to be underactive in humans who are depressed. The researchers saw neurons dying that make the neurotransmitters involved in emotion, pleasure, and cognition: norepinephrine, dopamine, and serotonin. Dosing the rats with an antidepressant significantly improved the brain-damaged areas and depressed behaviors.

Although antidepressants help, increasing levels of light during the day and having people with SAD sit in front of special lights is an effective treatment that has no side effects.

Or it could be a condition known as sundowning syndrome: the malaise, anxiety, confusion, and irritability that affect many people with dementia or Alzheimer's disease in the late afternoon. Experts aren't sure why. It could, like SAD, be connected to a body clock out of sync—to fatigue, stress, and failing vision. More than likely, it's a by-product of the brain disease that causes dementia.

Magnetic Energy May Work When Meds Fail

It sounds like science fiction, but magnetic energy stimulation might help the brains of the 40 percent of depressed people who don't respond to antidepressant medication. The treatment, called transcranial magnetic stimulation (TMS), activates neurons by sending pulses of magnetic energy into the brain.

It's approved by the Food and Drug Administration, and studies show it's safe and effective for some people. Psychiatrists at the University of Pennsylvania gave about forty minutes of TMS daily for four weeks to some three hundred patients with major depression who had failed to respond to medication and found they improved significantly with no major side effects. The magnetic field was delivered into the brain using small metallic coils attached to the scalp and positioned to target specific brain areas. In this study, they targeted a region of the prefrontal cortex known to be less active in depressed people. TMS is noninvasive and can be precisely aimed: it's been used to trigger ordinary people's inner mathematical savant, to invoke religious experiences, and it could be used to help people with other brain-based disorders such as schizophrenia, bipolar disorder, and Tourette's syndrome.

A Peak Time for Suicide

Early evening can be a peak time for suicide. Every day, approximately eighty Americans take their own life, and fifteen hundred more attempt to do so. In Italy, the hours between 4:00 P.M. and 7:00 P.M. are the riskiest for suicide for those between the ages of twenty-five and forty-four. In Tokyo, it's 6:00 P.M.

But predisposition and brain abnormalities may matter more than time of day. More than 60 percent of those who die by suicide have major depression. Low serotonin plays a role: it's known to be lacking in the brains of those who are depressed and those who are impulsive. Impulsiveness is a known factor in some suicides: many who survive say they changed their minds and opt to live after being interrupted in an attempt.

Among the brain regions of those who die by suicide that show changes are the orbital prefrontal cortex, which lies just above the eyes, and the dorsal raphe nucleus of the brain stem. The changes show problems making and using serotonin. Neurons in the dorsal raphe nucleus produce serotonin and have long projections that carry it to the orbital prefrontal cortex. But in those who die from suicide, the neurons of the raphe nucleus have more of the enzyme used to synthesize serotonin than brains of those who died of other causes, suggesting the brains of suicides are trying to make more serotonin.

Good Grief: Addicted to Grieving

Can't get over losing a loved one? For most people, time eventually heals the wounds. But 10 to 20 percent of the bereaved can't accept or get over the loss, even after years, a condition called complicated grief (CG). Researchers are finding this could be partly because in those with CG, reminders of the deceased activate the nucleus accumbens, a brain area associated with reward processing, pleasure, and addiction.

A team led by Mary-Frances O'Connor of the University of California, Los Angeles, studied functional magnetic resonance images of the brains of twenty-three women who had lost a mother or sister to breast cancer in the past five years. As they were scanned, the women saw pictures and words reminding them of their lost loved one, which activated brain networks associated with social pain in all of the women. But in the eleven women with CG, the images excited the nucleus accumbens as well, a part of the brain's reward circuit.

O'Connor believes this neural reward activity in response to memories of loved ones probably interferes with CG patients' adapting to loss: their brains still see these cues as predicting a rewarding experience, which activates the reward center. Scientists do not yet know why some people adapt better than others do.

6 *p.m.*

Coming Home

An Oxytocin High

Early evening is social time for your brain—a time to connect and reconnect. Maybe you're meeting good friends at that new restaurant or your family at home. You're happy to be seeing your partner, your kids, even Tabby and Spot. It gives your heart and your brain a little lift when you connect with your loved ones,. They make you feel good. It's oxytocin at work: the hormone of mother love, trust, and bonding.

Oxytocin is all about the positive side of personal interactions, and it works in many ways. Produced in the hypothalamus and secreted into the blood by the pituitary, it acts as both a hormone and a neurotransmitter. In women, oxytocin stimulates birth contractions, breast milk production, and bonding with baby. To encourage mammalian moms to attend to their offspring, oxytocin cooperates with dopamine in the deep midbrain regions associated with rewards. In both women and men, levels increase during sex and surge at orgasm, encouraging pair bonding and reinforcing those feelings of love. It's been dubbed the "cuddle hormone" (see "10:00 P.M."). And not surprisingly, scientists have found that oxytocin encourages feelings of trust. It literally feels good when someone seems to trust you, and this recognition motivates you to return that trust.

In a study of oxytocin effects, volunteers played a game in which they were asked to divide up a ten-dollar stake with a stranger. If the stranger accepted the split offer, both were paid, but if the offer was rejected, neither got anything. Those who inhaled a dose of oxytocin made offers that were 80 percent higher than those given a placebo. Moreover, subjects who received oxytocin did not demand more money than was offered. Researchers said the results suggest that oxytocin amplifies our generosity and empathy for others and motivates a desire to help them.

They also suggest that life experiences may retune your oxytocin mechanism to a different set point and even to different levels of trust. Living in a safe, nurturing environment might stimulate more oxytocin when we feel someone trusts us and stimulate us to return that trust. But stress, uncertainty, and isolation all work against the development of a trusting disposition.

Nobody Home? Loneliness Hurts

All the lonely people know it hurts, coming home to an empty house, having an empty social calendar, having an empty life, and for a long time, doctors have known it's not just your feelings. Being lonely can

---

PAT THE BUNNY—GO AHEAD. IT'S GOOD FOR YOUR BRAIN

Need some relief after that long commute, that blistering bus ride, that argument at the dry cleaner? Take some quality time with Tabby, Spot, or Long Ears. It's good for them and for your brain.

Many of us who found comfort as infants caressing fake furry friends in that ubiquitous board book have moved on to real live animal companions: some 100 million households in the United States have pets. Research shows that blood pressure and other stress indicators drop and that your brain sends out a burst of feel-good chemicals when you pet your own pets—but not when you pet others' animals. In tune with the times and busy schedules, researchers at the University of Missouri have been looking at human responses to a robot dog to see if mechanical pets can prompt the same good response.

make you physically sick. The reason, they are discovering, is that chronic loneliness triggers a change in gene activity.

Researcher Steven Cole of the University of California, Los Angeles, and colleagues looked at results of the UCLA Loneliness Scale, a self-administered psychiatric questionnaire for measuring that emotion. They found that those who score in the top 15 percent are at greater risk for illness, with increased gene activity linked to inflammation (a measure of illness and risk of illness) and reduced gene activity associated with antibody production and antiviral responses (the activities that protect against illness). Researchers say these patterns of gene expression were specific to loneliness, not to any other negative feelings such as depression, but they weren't sure why.

A CLOSE CIRCLE OF FRIENDS

Sure, family matters. But an Australian study shows that our friends seem to matter even more—so much more that having and holding onto friendships enhances and prolongs healthy life.

The decade-long Australian Longitudinal Study of Aging, which was begun in 1992, concentrated on the social environment, general health, lifestyle, and age of death of 1,477 persons seventy years or older. They were asked how much personal and telephone contact they had with friends, children, relatives, and acquaintances.

To the researchers' surprise, it turned out that regardless of socioeconomic status, health, and way of life, friendships increased life expectancy to a much greater extent than, say, frequent contact with children and other relatives. And this was true even after these friends had moved away to another city.

A Harvard School of Public Health study found friendship is good for the heart when it looked at older men. Those with an extended set of connections had considerably smaller amounts of a molecule called interleukin-6 in their blood than in that of loners. High levels of interleukin-6 are a risk factor for heart disease.

In a new study of 1,023 Taiwanese adults, Cole got a clearer idea when he analyzed data from a variety of lonely people and found that their cortisol hormone wasn't doing its job of suppressing the genes associated with inflammation. Recent animal studies from Cole's group confirm the link: cortisol receptors stopped working in rhesus monkeys that were socially stressed.

The loneliness research continues. Cole and his colleagues are now working with patients in Chicago to see how different degrees of loneliness affect health.

Oh, Those Comforting Cravings. Or Is It Addiction?

Your brain is happy to have that first drink of the evening. It's part of leisure time with friends and family. But if your best friends and family are named Johnny Walker, Jack Daniels, or Grey Goose, you may be in trouble.

And what's in your glass may be the result of what's in your genes. There's no doubt that some of us can't take it or leave it: 8.5 percent of American adults have an alcohol issue, and about 2 percent have substance abuse problems with hard drugs and are also likely alcoholics. And some who came of age in the Age of Aquarius still like to have a little cannabis puff or cocaine snort. (See "Still Crazy After All These Years?" page 122.)

Addiction sure starts out feeling good most times, but like a bad love affair you can't shake, it ends up being so much of a good thing that it goes bad.

Addiction is a chronic brain disease characterized by compulsive substance seeking and use, despite harmful consequences, says the National Institute on Drug Abuse. It's a destructive reward-and-repeat-and-relapse action that changes a brain, body, and life.

At the heart of all addictions is dopamine: the neurotransmitter that allows us to experience pleasure and calibrates our reward center to motivate us toward actions that trigger a reward response. Many biologically useful actions and substances such as orgasm, breastfeeding, and food prime the dopamine pumps. (See "Noon.")

But addictive drugs and alcohol can actually physically change the pleasure pathways and max out that response. Drugs such as cocaine and heroin commandeer the reward circuit, prompting very large and very fast dopamine surges into the nucleus accumbens. Your brain very reasonably copes with this dopamine tidal wave by reducing the amount of dopamine receptors so it won't be overwhelmed. That sets up a vicious feedback loop: the fewer the receptors, the more dopamine it takes to get high, and the more receptors are cut back, and the more addictive substance it takes to make more dopamine. And so on. Alcohol has a similar effect, but through a different mechanism, involving gamma-aminobutyric acid (GABA) and glutamate.

Ongoing abuse of all of these substances changes the actual neurons in the system. This explains why it takes increasing amounts of the addictive source to get high, why it's so hard to quit, and why addicts eventually lose the ability to feel any pleasure.

Bottoms Up: Where Many Alcoholics End

Heavy drinkers tend to have a slight feeling of superiority over drug addicts. For sure, alcohol is a more socially acceptable addiction, and it's legal and readily available at a reasonable cost. But in spite of all the research showing moderate drinking has benefits, alcohol in large amounts is not good for your brain or body. It destroys liver and brain function and contributes to risky or negligent acts that range from dangerous falls to homicide.

It's estimated that genes contribute half of the risk of becoming an alcoholic: alcoholism runs in families (it gallops in some), and some ethnic and racial groups are more susceptible than others to the effects of alcohol. Researchers are still working on the exact pathways for alcohol addiction and intoxication. They know it involves and confuses GABA, which carries signals between certain nerve cells; glutamate, our major excitatory neurotransmitter; and, of course, dopamine.

What they do know in unappetizing detail is that drinking large amounts of alcohol kills off newborn neurons in a developing fetus, shrinks adult brains, and is connected with serious mental and neurological problems. We all know the social and personal costs.

Is Addiction the Result Rather Than the Cause of Brain Damage?

Scientists know that substance abuse damages the brain. But research suggests that in some people, that "damage" may have already been there and may actually fuel addiction.

Chronic drug users seem to have fewer dopamine D2 receptors in the reward pathways of their brain, which often makes them less sensitive to natural pleasures such as food and sex. Scientists believe this could reinforce addiction by causing users to seek from drugs what they can't get naturally—the "high" caused by a surge of dopamine—and that some people may be born with an abnormally low D2 receptor count.

Jeffrey Dalley and his colleagues at the Cambridge University in the United Kingdom compared the brains of six impulsive rats to six normal rats and then allowed the animals to self-administer cocaine.

HOW ALCOHOL STEALS YOUR SENSE OF HUMOR (WHAT? YOU DON'T FIND THAT FUNNY?)

Alcoholics have trouble understanding jokes, which hints they may be missing out on much more than a chance to laugh.

German neuroscientists showed twenty-nine alcoholics and twenty-nine healthy control subjects the introduction to a joke and then a choice of punch lines—only one of which made logical sense and was funny. Only 68 percent of the alcoholics chose the correct punch line compared to 92 percent of nondrinkers.

An alcoholic's problems with social cues are consistent with the frontal lobe hypothesis, which postulates that damage to the prefrontal cortex, known to be vulnerable to alcohol's toxic effects, leads to behavioral deficits. Most other studies of alcoholics' brain function have concentrated on perceptual problems caused by such damage. But people who have problems with social cognition have difficulty getting along with other people.

The impulsive rats became addicted more quickly than their nonimpulsive labmates, and they showed a significantly lower number of D2 receptors in a brain region associated with reward anticipation and craving.

But the researchers found no differences in the dorsolateral striatum, where a decrease in D2 receptors is seen most commonly after habitual drug use. That, they said, suggests that progressive drug use produces progressive changes in the brain. Having fewer D2 receptors may predispose them to high levels of impulsiveness, which may lead to experimentation with drugs. Long-term drug abuse, in turn, may cause damage in parts of the brain's reward pathway, causing addicts to compulsively seek out drugs.

Still Crazy After All These Years? Aging Isn't Stopping Drug Use

Cartoons in the 1960s showed the future: Grandma and Grandpa passing the time in their rockers, passing a joint back and forth as they recall their pot-smoking days in Haight-Ashbury.

Back then, researchers were convinced people would "grow out of" recreational drug use as they aged. Turns out they were wrong and the cartoonists were right. Boomers, the generation born between 1946 and 1964, are clinging to recreational drug use as they line up for Medicare. In fact, it seems their drug use is way higher than for previous generations, according to the National Institute on Drug Abuse.

Boomers already make up 29 percent of the U.S. population. By 2030 there will be 71 million people aged sixty-five and older. That's a significant percentage of the population getting high—and on Medicare.

Researchers G. J. Dowling, Susan R. B. Weiss, and Timothy P. Condon looked at hospital records for people for people aged fifty-five and older who sought emergency room treatment and mentioned using various drugs. Cocaine mentions rose from 1,400 in 1995 to almost 5,000 in 2002, an increase of 240 percent. Heroin increased from 1,300 to 3,400 (160 percent), marijuana from 300 to 1,700 (467 percent), and amphetamines from 70 to 560 (700 percent). In 2002, the National Survey on Drug Use and Health found some 2.7 percent of adults between fifty and fifty-nine had used recreational drugs at least once in the preceding year. By 2005, that number had jumped to 4.4 percent.

So that's the problem with elder drug use? There can be health consequences for the imbibers and the Medicare system. Continued drug use may strain those aging brains, especially systems involving the neurotransmitters dopamine, serotonin, and glutamate and GABA, which all change with age.

Aging brains already show many losses similar to the effects of cocaine-induced injury: some loss of motor and cognitive functioning. Seniors who use cocaine could be compounding the damage. Aging also leads to changes in metabolic rates and, in particular, in the processes whereby a drug is absorbed, distributed, metabolized, and eliminated. Add alcohol, and the changes can have devastating consequences.

But researchers really don't know the true extent of the problem, since doctors may not be asking elders about drugs. They assume—falsely—that seniors don't use recreational drugs.

7 p.m.

Gotta Sing, Gotta Dance

It's evening after a long day, and your brain wants music. Maybe you put on a CD, or turn on your MP3 player, or you go out to hear live music at a concert or a dance club.

Country, folk, jazz, or opera: your brain loves music. It likes it so much that it wants music all day long: music surrounds us at home, in the car, in shops, on the street, even in elevators. It provides the background score to movies and screenplays—and to your life. A symphony can move us to tears, rock and roll gets our feet flying, and lullabies put us to sleep. Parents everywhere croon soothingly to babies.

Brain scans prove that music is irresistible, and possibly addictive. When scientists scanned brains that were moved to emotion by music, they found that music activated some of the same reward systems as food, sex, and addictive drugs. No wonder "sex, drugs, and rock and roll" is a catchphrase: it appears that your brain likes them all in the same place.

Our fondness for music has deep roots. People in every known society have been making music since the dawn of culture. More than thirty thousand years ago, early humans were already playing bone flutes, percussive instruments, and jaw harps and dancing to both tunes and rhythms. We seem to be born with it: babies as young as two months turn toward pleasant sounds and away from dissonant ones.

The Musical Path to the Brain

As researchers learn more about where music lives in our brain, they are finding there is no specialized center for music. It tickles our limbic center, but it's all through the brain, including areas that are usually involved in other kinds of cognition, which helps explain how and why it moves us so.

It enters through the ear, of course. The ear has the fewest sensory cells of any sensory organ—thirty-five hundred inner hair cells occupy the ear versus 100 million photoreceptors in the eye. Yet our mental response to music is remarkably adaptable; even a little study can "retune" the way the brain handles musical inputs.

Research finds that music and language share much: both are a means of communication, and each has syntax, a set of rules that govern the proper combination of elements (notes and words, respectively). Some imaging findings suggest that a region in the frontal lobe helps structure the syntax of both music and language, while other parts of the brain handle related aspects of language and music processing.

The psychologist Oliver Sacks suggests that music occupies more areas of our brain than language does. Imaging studies of the brain's responses to music, and to sounds in general, show that the active areas are related to your individual experiences and (not surprisingly) to your musical training.

Music Survives Brain Damage

Our appreciation of music is so deep that it can survive even when the brain is injured. Scientists have found that those so incapacitated by stroke or other brain damage that they can't walk, read, or even tie their shoes respond to music, and in some cases, depending on the area that is injured, they can still make music.

Before modern imaging techniques were available, scientists learned much about the brain's inner musical workings mainly by studying famous composers who had suffered brain damage. They found that French composer Maurice Ravel retained much of his musicality even after he began to show symptoms in 1933 of what they think

HOW THE BRAIN HEARS OVER DIN

How can your brain pick out a single conversation when music is blaring and people are singing? The brain hears more than we know: it can selectively discard what doesn't seem relevant. At a crowded restaurant, it seems as if it would be hard to hear the person you're talking to over the clinking glasses and silverware, the chatter and laughter. But somehow your brain filters out all the noise.

Scientists have known about this useful ability for more than fifty years. In fact, it's called the *cocktail party effect*. But they're still trying to figure out how the brain does it. A study in the journal *Public Library of Science Biology* hints at an answer.

Neuroscientists played one repeating tone to volunteers, along with a bunch of louder, distracting tones of different pitches. The participants pressed a button if they heard the repeating tone. Meanwhile, the researchers were monitoring the subjects' brain activity. It turns out that even when the subjects didn't think they could detect the repeating tone, it still traveled from the inner ear to the auditory cortex. Somewhere after that initial processing, it got discarded before the person was consciously aware of it. So all of those other conversations at a crowded breakfast table probably make it into your brain, but they get thrown away before you're aware of them.

Unless, of course, you're eavesdropping.

---

was focal cerebral degeneration, or brain tissue atrophy. He could no longer write music, but he could still hear and remember his old compositions and play scales. His situation added to the theory that music might not be in any one part of the brain.

The illness of another composer suggested that music and speech are processed independently. After a stroke in 1953, the Russian composer Vissarion Shebalin could no longer talk or understand speech, yet he was able to write music until his death ten years later.

In another case, a woman who had damage to both temporal lobes (including the auditory cortical regions) could not recognize any music. Nevertheless, she had normal emotional reactions to different types of music, and her ability to match an emotion with a particular musical selection was completely normal. This suggests the temporal lobe is needed to comprehend melody but not to produce an emotional reaction.

Music "hath charms to soothe the savage breast," wrote English dramatist William Congreve. Indeed, it can elicit strong emotions, since the brain's limbic system is intensely involved. We all know it affects moods, soothing the depressed and manic alike or prompting a cheery outlook. It is used as a therapy to comfort the chronically and terminally ill and to help ease pain and stress.

Recent research shows it is also good for the body. A study showed music significantly lower blood pressure in people with hypertension who listen for thirty minutes a day to classical, Celtic, or raga (Indian) music.

Your Brain Expands to Store Music

Of course, your brain's response to music depends on your exposure to music and musical training. But even a little training can quickly change your brain.

Studies of musicians dramatically confirm that the brain can revise its wiring to support musical activities. Musicians, who usually practice many hours a day for years, show such effects: their responses to music differ from those of nonmusicians. They also have much more development in certain areas in their brains. Imaging has shown the volume of the auditory cortex in some musicians to be 130 percent larger than in the rest of us, with the percentages of volume increase linked to levels of musical training, suggesting that learning music proportionally increases the number of neurons that process it.

Studies confirm that the brain can revise its wiring to support musical activities (and presumably other activities) when performed repeatedly. Researchers find that prolonged learning produces marked responses and physical changes in the brain, with musicians' brains devoting more area toward motor control of the fingers used to play a specific instrument.

So You Think You Can Dance?

Your brain is just itching to take you dancing tonight, whether it's a ballroom dance class, a jazz aerobics workout, or just a toe-tapping bop across the living room floor to your favorite CD. To your conscious self, this is just a satisfyingly rhythmic hop, skip, and pirouette. To your brain, it's a neurochemical ballet, with the invisible choreography in your brain as intricate as that for any cast-of-hundreds Broadway showstopper.

Here's the short and simple version. Your brain has to figure out spatial awareness, balance, and timing. The posterior parietal cortex (a region toward the back of the brain) busily translates visual information into motor commands, sending signals forward to motion planning areas in the premotor cortex and the primary motor cortex, which generates neural impulses that travel to the spinal cord and on to the muscles to make them contract. Voilà: you dance.

At the same time, sensory receptors in the muscles are giving feedback about your exact orientation in space through nerves that pass through the spinal cord to the cerebral cortex. Subcortical circuits in the cerebellum at the back of the brain and in the basal ganglia at the brain's core also help to update motor commands based on sensory feedback and refine our actual motions. And this is how you execute those more demanding movement, such as that pirouette.

There's lots more. Some surprising parts of the brain get involved, including a region in the right hemisphere that corresponds to Broca's area in the frontal lobe's left hemisphere. Broca's area is associated with speech production (which, actually, is not that much of a surprise after all). The finding of Broca's area's involvement supports a theory of language evolution that proposes language evolved from a gesture system before becoming vocal, and dance is a gesture language.

Born to Rock?

Although many of us think we're not musical, studies of babies show that just isn't so. Babies as young as two months react to music.

Perhaps that's why we instinctively croon in a musical manner, using wide ranges of pitch and melodic-like phrases, often called *motherese.* It seems that all cultures use motherese, and babies not only react positively but appear to encourage the performance in their mothers. In one study, North American and East Indian mothers were recorded singing the same song with their infant present and then without their baby. Others listening to the moms' recordings were able to judge accurately when the baby was present.

The study also showed that at least some musical cues appear to play across cultures: listeners to the recordings could accurately tell from a mom's voice if her baby had been present, whether they heard the song in their own language or in another.

The Creative Brain

If you're not busy dancing, you may be heading out at this hour to one of your favorite things: your painting, quilting, or flower arranging class; your banjo lesson; or choir practice. Some of us are writing

---

TANGO TO BETTER BALANCE

Tango, it seems, can help improve balance in people with Parkinson's disease and in the elderly.

Parkinson's disease stems from a loss of neurons in the basal ganglia, a problem that interrupts messages meant for the motor cortex, and causes tremors, rigidity, and difficulty initiating movements. Gammon M. Earhart and Madeleine E. Hackney of the Washington University School of Medicine in St. Louis found that after twenty tango classes, study subjects "froze" less often. Compared with subjects who attended an exercise class instead, the tango dancers also had better balance and higher scores on the Get Up and Go test, which identifies those at risk for falling.

In another study, seniors aged sixty-two to ninety who had fallen within the previous year were assigned to two hours of tango lessons for ten weeks or to a walking class for the same period. At the end of the study, the dancers performed significantly better at walking and balance than the walkers.

a novel or retiring to the garage to work on that classic car, design a custom bookcase, or make a model aircraft.

Most of us, mindful of being mocked, modestly call these activities *hobbies, pastimes,* or *projects.* But many times, we're exercising our creativity in the challenges these activities offer: the ability to solve problems and go beyond traditional ideas and relationships to find and create meaningful new ideas, forms, or actions.

The creative process and the scientific understanding of creativity are far from complete. But one truth is clear: creativity is not a rare gift from the gods. We can call it up from within us in surprising ways.

Research is showing, for example, that a musical ear, once thought to be inborn, can be learned, and that the brain expands in areas related to learned musical expertise. (See "The Musical Ear Is Learned, Not Born," page 132.) Creativity, it seems, is within the grasp of most of us, and not just the talented few.

Not every one of us is a potential genius or great artist, of course. But we can buff up our creative potential through exercise, attitudes, and environment—the same factors that help us maximize our physical and mental muscles. We can all experience creativity and express it in varying ways.

Scientists have had a hard time pinning down the creative process in the brain because problem solving and other mentally creative activities take place over time and involve many parts of the brain (and body).

Right Brain, Left Brain?

Creativity isn't only, or even, about intelligence. Experts say it's based more on the ability to think outside usual rules and guidelines, called divergent thinking. That ability seems to reside more in the right hemisphere of the brain, which tends to be more intuitive, abstract, and imaginative. The left hemisphere is more detail oriented, analytical, logical, and verbal, called convergent thinking.

Creative and productive people use both sides of the brain: we need the solid grounding of convergent (merging) thinking to provide a base for the inspirational imagination of divergent (differing) thinking. But apparently the left brain can block the creative right side: patients who have damage or dementia in the left frontal lobe damage can become amazingly artistic and creative.

As scientists continue to explore the roots of creativity, they've discovered one clue: numerous artists and scientists have said that creative revelations often come when they aren't trying—when they were involved in unrelated tasks, idly daydreaming, or after sleep. It worked for both Einstein and Dalí. So maybe a little break will work for you too.

Don't Oversimplify That Right Brain Stuff

Scores of popular books have seized on this purported schism in your head. Artist and psychologist Betty Edwards's popular book of thirty years ago, *Drawing on the Right Side of the Brain,* is still touting the benefits of more creative, right-brained forms of artistic expression.

Yet the left-brained-versus-right-brained dichotomy is grossly oversimplified. For one thing, this distinction implies that people who are verbally gifted are not likely to be artistically talented, but research suggests otherwise. Moreover, neuroscience studies suggest that the brain's two hemispheres work in a highly coordinated fashion.

Like many other brain myths, this one contains a kernel of truth. For several decades beginning in the 1960s, neuroscientist Roger Sperry of the California Institute of Technology, psychologist Michael S. Gazzaniga of the University of California, Santa Barbara, and their colleagues studied patients who underwent surgery to sever the corpus callosum (the large band of neural fibers connecting the two hemispheres) in an effort to control intractable epilepsy. (See the box in the Introduction called "Do You Need Only Half a Brain?" on page 7.)

The research showed that the left and right hemispheres are indeed different. In most of us, the left hemisphere is specialized for most aspects of language, whereas the right hemisphere is specialized for most visuospatial skills. Further research has confirmed that your brain does indeed specialize—to some point, that is. The right hemisphere, for example, tends to play a larger role than the left does in interpreting the vocal tone of spoken language. But these right-left brain differences are only relative. And because practically all of us have an intact corpus callosum, our hemispheres are continually communicating and interacting.

The Musical Ear Is Learned, Not Born

Here's news for those who believe creativity is inborn. For music, at least, researchers find by looking at brains listening to Bach that there is evidence that it's practice, training, and experience, not genes, that develop a musical ear.

Researchers used functional magnetic resonance imaging (fMRI) to examine the effect of music on the brains of experienced musicians. They found trained musicians had more extensive and complex neural responses to music played on their instrument of expertise than on another instrument. They had highly trained classical musicians who played the flute or the violin listen to two familiar Bach selections while they were scanned and recorded brain activity. If musical talent is innate, the researchers would expect to see all classical musicians engage a brain network specific to classical music, regardless of their instrument of expertise. But the musicians showed significantly different brain responses to different instruments. When the violinists listened to the violin and the flutists listened to the flute, they engaged many more areas of the brain—areas related to sense of self, motor control, and suppression of unwanted movements.

Movement researchers have found similar results when dancers watched dancing: their brains responded to dances they had mastered.

8 p.m.

Humor Is Healthy

Time for your favorite sitcom? Go ahead: laugh. It's good for you. Watching that sitcom isn't a waste of time: you may be tuning up your brain and your health. Humor can improve your memory, your immune system, the oxygen supply to your brain, your social life, and your mood.

Here are just a few good things a good laugh does for you: it prompts your pituitary gland to release its own opiates, which suppress pain; it suppresses your stress chemicals, cortisol and epinephrine; and it increases both antibodies and natural killer cells. Humor helps us remember, several studies show. When researchers read a list of thirty words to a group and showed some of them a funny video clip afterward, those who had seen the video remembered 20 percent more than those who had not.

The Best Medicine

It could be that laughter is medicine. The case of editor and writer Norman Cousins has entered mythology, but it's true. When he was diagnosed in the 1960s with a degenerative kind of arthritis and was unable to get any pain relief, he created his own therapy: laughter and massive doses of Vitamin C. Cousins spent hours every day watching comedy movies and reading humor books, and after several months, he said he was nearly pain free. He lived until 1990, detailing his personal prescription in the best seller *Anatomy of an Illness*.

Some in the medical profession agree. Dr. Hunter Campbell "Patch" Adams became known for dressing as a clown and promoting humor in the hospital. He has been the subject of a movie and every year leads a group that dress as clowns to bring humor to patients.

There's even a name for the study of humor and laughter: *gelotology*, from the Greek *gelos*, for laughter.

Tracking Your Internal Laugh Track

Where does your brain register laughter? In more than one place, it seems, including our pleasure center. Sarcasm, however, has a completely different address.

Researchers at Dartmouth College's Center for Cognitive Neuroscience used functional magnetic resonance imaging (fMRI) to scan volunteers as they watched episodes of *Seinfeld* or *The Simpsons*. The investigators found that humor detection lit up the left inferior frontal and posterior temporal cortices—the left side of the thinking brain. Humor appreciation, in contrast, provoked activity in the bilateral regions of the insular cortex and the amygdala—the emotional areas deeper inside. Research has shown that the left inferior frontal cortex is involved in reconciling ambiguous meanings with prior knowledge. And ambiguity, incongruity, and surprise are key elements in many jokes.

Sarcasm, however, is more complex and appears to take up more brain real estate. Researchers looking at sarcasm recognition in those with frontotemporal dementia and Alzheimer's disease found those who had trouble recognizing sarcasm (but not sincere statements) had problems with parts of the orbitofrontal cortex, the insula, and the amygdala on the right side of the brain. Another study showed sarcasm involves the anterior cingulated. Recognizing sarcasm, the researchers noted, is a complex process involving more social messages (and conflicting messages at that) than humor.

Yet other studies have shown that parts of our pleasure center, the nucleus accumbens and the amygdala, get involved in humor, too. Could it be humor is yet another addiction?

THE AHA! MOMENT

So how do we know when someone gets the joke? Simple: the eyes have it.

We've all experienced the aha! moment when a joke suddenly makes sense and nonsense, and we are amused. Scientists have long tried to figure out what is happening in our brain during that crucial split second. Now a researcher at the University of Michigan at Ann Arbor has found a window into that state of mind: the eyes. Our pupils, he says, dilate the moment we realize a joke is funny.

Humor psychologist Richard Lewis (no relation to the comedian) showed volunteers cartoons from the *New Yorker* magazine and used an eye-tracking device to monitor pupil dilation and eye movements. Lewis found that pupils dilated about a half-second after their gaze fell on the regions of a cartoon that were critical to humor—a period similar to the time it takes our brain to derive meaning from words we read.

His work could help researchers investigating humor-related brain activity with magnetic resonance imaging or an electroencephalograph (EEG). So far it appears we do not have a distinct neurological funny bone. But they haven't figured out why we have a sense of humor in the first place.

TV Addiction Is No Mere Metaphor

Where is your brain most evenings? Is it hooked on the small screen? Are you eschewing other activities, unable to lift your eyes from the program to even take a phone call? Maybe your brain is programmed to be addicted to TV.

No doubt the world's most popular leisure pastime is television. We might bemoan the waste of time spent viewing, but we still spend major evening hours on the sofa with the remote control: on average, three hours a day—half our leisure time and more than any other single activity except for work and sleep.

Even researchers who study TV for a living marvel at the medium's hold on them personally. Percy Tannenbaum of the University of California at Berkeley has written, "Among life's more embarrassing moments have been countless occasions when I am engaged in conversation in a room while a TV set is on, and I cannot for the life of me stop from periodically glancing over to the screen. This occurs not only during dull conversations but during reasonably interesting ones just as well."

There's a reason your brain keeps pushing your eyes back to that television screen, and it isn't about the content; it's about neurobiology. It's the medium, not the message.

Most research has been focused on content, looking for a relationship between TV violence and real-life violence. But our compulsion to view seems to spring from our biological "orienting response": our instinctive visual or auditory reaction to any sudden or novel stimulus. It is part of our evolutionary heritage, a built-in sensitivity to detect movement and potential threats from predators.

The typical orienting reactions include dilation of the blood vessels to your brain, a slowing of heartbeats, and constriction of blood vessels to major muscle groups. Brain alpha waves are blocked for a few seconds, and your body quiets while your brain focuses its attention on gathering more information.

Decades ago, researchers found that the so-called formal features of television—cuts, edits, zooms, pans, sudden noises—activate this orienting response, keeping our attention on the screen. By watching how brain waves were affected by these editing and style techniques, the researchers concluded that it's the form, not the content, of television that is unique.

And yes—it dulls your brain. Researchers have studied reactions to TV using a variety of instruments including EEG to measure the brain waves, skin resistance, and heart rate of TV viewers. Some people were also given beepers, and if they were beeped when watching TV, they reported feeling relaxed and passive.

The EEG studies backed that up, showing less mental stimulation during viewing than during reading. What was more surprising was that the sense of relaxation ended when the set was turned off, but the feelings of passivity and lowered alertness continued.

When surveyed, people have said they felt television somehow sucked out their energy, leaving them with more trouble concentrating after viewing than before. Heavy viewers reported feeling more anxious than light viewers when in unstructured situations, and they are more easily bored and distracted. In fact, some have connected overly sensitive orienting response to attention deficit hyperactivity disorder. They also report withdrawal feelings when they stop viewing or cut back, a sure sign to some of addiction.

Part 5

2
3
4

Winding Down
Fear, Sex, Sleep, and Dreams
9 P.M. to Midnight

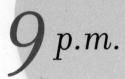

9 p.m.

Things That Go Bump in the Night

Is that a strange footstep in the hall, a face at the window, a rattle of a doorknob in the dark? Is there danger out there—or worse, in here? Your amygdala wants to know.

Fear, along with hunger and anger, is one of your brain's primitive and primary survival mechanisms. It's hard-wired into us and most other daytime animals. Since primeval times, humans have been vulnerable to night-stalking predators. The night is also prime time for human-on-human violence, especially domestic violence. Government crime reports show that the risk of domestic violence is highest between the hours of 4:00 P.M. and midnight, with sexual assaults peaking between 8:00 P.M. and 2:00 A.M.

How Fear Works in Your Brain

Fear is a physical reaction to danger that triggers a neurochemical alarm throughout your body and brain. When your senses perceive what could be a threat—say, a strange face at the kitchen window in the dark—the information ricochets through several centers in your brain. It's a collaborative effort, with the most active player your sentry and protector: the poised-for-fight-or-flight amygdala. Neuroscientist Joseph E. LeDoux, a pioneer in the study of fear, describes it as the hub in the brain's wheel of fear.

The danger data race from the thalamus (the brain's receiver of information from the senses), to the amygdala through the cortex (the seat of reasoning that analyzes data) and/or the hippocampus (the memory input center that compares the new information to past experiences), while your hypothalamus tells the adrenal and pituitary to pour cortisol and other stress hormones into the mix.

Your amygdala is fast: it has its pistol out of the holster (enemy at the window!) before the thinking brain can chime in (it's your neighbor looking for her cat). It takes only twelve milliseconds for the thalamus to alert the amygdala, says LeDoux, who calls this emotional brain reaction the "low road." The "high road," or the trip through the thinking brain and hippocampus, takes two or three times as long to process the input and send it back to the amygdala.

When the danger is direct and real, this hair-trigger fear response is an important protection. But sometimes your brain can overdo it, as news reports of accidental shootings and other overreactions show. An extreme, immediate, and misplaced attack response to fear has led to tragic mistakes.

The after-effects of fear may linger long after danger is gone. After a scare, you may find yourself opening closets, looking under beds, triple-checking door locks, sleeping with 911 on speed dial, and taking other unnecessary precautions. An extreme reaction is posttraumatic stress disorder.

Unrelenting fear is a brother to stress, setting off the same neurochemical and physical events, and it can lead to similar physical and mental ills. (See "10:0o A.M.") When fear is still standing guard long after the danger is gone, you may develop a phobia or other anxiety disorder.

There's no single fear gene, but studies show that identical twins—even those who grow up separately—share more fears than fraternal twins do.

Who's Afraid? Not These Brain Cells

Researchers have been working on ways to free people from ongoing fears, especially irrational fear. A range of medications and talk therapies helps some people, but retraining the brain or targeting neurons could be more effective.

It seems there are neurons responsible for helping people overcome fear of things they once found scary: intercalated cells, which could be an off switch for the ever-alert amygdala. Scientists trained two rat populations, one with intercalated cells in the amygdala intact and the other with them disabled, to be afraid at a certain sound by giving them a mild shock every time it was played. After awhile, the animals would freeze in their tracks when they heard the noise, bracing for pain. The team then played the tone without the shock. When they sounded the note again a week later, rats with healthy intercalated cells weren't bothered, whereas the others froze. The scientists believe that the intercalated cells form what they call "extinction memories," which associate a once-feared stimulus, such as an air raid siren or a car backfiring, with a harmless outcome.

The finding by Rutgers University scientists could pave the way for these cells in the amygdala to become drug targets for treating phobias as well as posttraumatic stress disorder in soldiers and others.

When the Brain Decides It's Time to Scram

It seems that your brain has two ways to respond to danger, and it's all about how immediate the danger is: if the threat is far away, it strategizes; if it's nearby, it reacts. This setup allows your brain to choose the response best for its survival, say researchers at the University College London's imaging neuroscience department who used a video game and functional magnetic resonance imaging (fMRI) scans to study responses to threats.

The scans showed that when a fear-provoking stimulus (say, a bear) is detected in the distance, the human brain switches on circuitry that analyzes the threat level and ways to avoid harm. Should the bear move closer, increasing the threat, other regions of the brain jump into action, triggering an immediate fight, flight, or freeze response.

The Pac-Man–like video game required fourteen subjects to move game pieces along a virtual grid to avoid a virtual predator. To

TIME SEEMS TO STAND STILL IN FEAR

When a car skids on black ice, or when the Tiffany vase is in mid-fall to the marble floor, or when you watch the north tower go up in flames, time appears to go in slow motion.

We'd swear our brains perceive time differently during crisis, but is it true? Scientists at the Baylor College of Medicine in Houston say it isn't so: perception remains the same whether we're lounging by the fireside or being attacked by a bison.

They tested this by having twenty volunteers free-fall 150 feet into a net. To test for visual distortion caused by slowed perception of a terrifying fall, researchers strapped chronometers onto subjects' wrists and flashed numbers too fast to read. They theorized that if we actually see more due to slowed time, the fallers should be able to read the numbers in the midst of disaster. But they could not.

It seems that during a frightening event, your amygdala kicks in and lays down an extra set of memories. The more memory you have of an event, the longer you believe it took.

increase the fear factor, players snagged by predators could receive a series of three slight electric shocks, a slight shock, or no punishment at all.

The fMRIs of the participants' brains as they played showed that when a predator was a distance away, there was increased activity in brain areas responsible for more sophisticated processing, such as the ventromedial prefrontal cortex (VMPFC), a section of the cortex. As the predator moved closer, the periaqueductal gray (PAG) area of the brain, located near the brain stem, kicked into action. The PAG, which triggers the release of opioid analgesics, the body's internal painkiller, also handles more visceral reactions such as freezing in response to a scare, and the fight-or-flight response.

When there was the threat of more shocks, researcher saw more activity in the PAG, but the threat of fewer shocks increased activity in the VMPFC, says study coauthor Dean Mobbs.

Overactive PAGs (and underactive VMPFCS) could play a role in panic disorders; the reverse—deficient PAGs and hyper VMPFCS—may lead to anxiety.

The Many Parts of a Violent Brain

That car just cut you off, and without a signal or a hesitation, causing you to slam on the brakes in your car, spilling groceries all over the back seat, and setting off some road rage sparks in your brain.

Anger is no stranger in your head. You may fly into a rage, hurl curses, slam the steering wheel with your fist, and scream death threats, but you (and most of us) do not usually escalate to commit violence on another. Or do you?

A random violent act may proceed from your brain into action, but for most of us, it's a rarity. For criminals who repeat violent acts, it's something else: a state of damaged mind and possibly a damaged brain.

Researchers say that it takes a stew of ingredients to make a violent criminal. Violent behavior is the result of a complex combination of biology and environment, including gender, genetics, brain anatomy, biochemistry, and a traumatic childhood. Testosterone is involved (see "The Testosterone Connection" on the following page). In general, men are more primed for aggression than women and commit most violent crimes. But it takes more than gender to make a person violent, and it's related more to poor impulse control than pure evil.

Studies have connected antisocial behavior with one version of the gene for monoamine oxidase A, an enzyme that breaks down serotonin and other mood chemicals—at least in men who were abused as children. Other research shows that neglect and abuse in childhood may permanently reduce serotonin levels. In men with this violence-linked version of the gene, areas of the brain that govern emotion are smaller, the amygdala becomes more active when they are shown angry and fearful faces, and the brain regions that regulate fear are less active.

Other studies using positron emission tomography scans have found lower levels of activity in the frontal brain regions of murderers than in the general population. People with abnormalities in this part of the thinking brain may have real problems showing restraint. Researchers think the orbitofrontal cortex, an area involved in decision making, usually puts the brakes on the limbic system, especially the

---

THE TESTOSTERONE CONNECTION

It's the punch line to many a joke, but it has a basis in fact: testosterone does contribute to aggression, especially in males, who have much higher levels of it than females.

The association is more obvious in other animal species. In humans overall, the association seems slight. Testosterone levels can fluctuate widely. They increase in men, for example, just before competitive sports and remain high for some time in the winners but decrease rapidly in losers. That seems to suggest that constant competition and conflict could permanently change a testosterone level.

Researchers have found significantly higher levels of testosterone in violent offenders as compared with nonviolent criminals. And in general, male testosterone levels peak in the late teens and remain high until the mid-twenties—exactly the age group in which male aggression and violence are most common.

Information on testosterone in women is inconclusive, which is not surprising since women synthesize only a small fraction as much as men, and female violent offenders are rare. But when James Dabbs and his colleagues at Georgia State University measured testosterone in eighty-seven women at a maximum-security prison, they found that the hormone levels varied with the violence of the women's crimes and their behavior behind bars. The most violent women, who also showed the greatest aggression toward other inmates, had the most testosterone.

amygdala, where fear and aggression arise. A brain defect that blocks this communication might leave someone unable to control emotional reactions.

One of the earliest documented examples of the importance of the orbitofrontal cortex is that of the nineteenth-century railworker Phineas Gage, who had an iron bar blasted into his skull. Gage survived the accident but underwent dramatic personality changes, becoming moody, uninhibited, antisocial, and belligerent. Later studies determined the iron bar had most likely damaged his prefrontal cortex.

Damage to the hippocampus can interfere with processing emotional information, and a malfunction of the amygdala could underlie violent behavior. This theory could explain the lack of fear, empathy, and regret in criminals who plan their acts and commit them in cold blood.

Learned gender roles play a part too: boys are taught to fight back, girls to play nice. Learned social roles, for example, growing up in an abusive childhood where violence is the norm, also contribute.

The mystery is why some people are able to overcome terrible childhood experiences or even early brain damage, and others cannot and become violent offenders.

10 p.m.

Lust, Sex, and Love

As the hour turns late, thoughts, feelings, and neurochemicals turn to romance. Or lust.

Right about now, you've got that loving feeling. Your brain is probably thinking about sex—and perhaps helping your body perform it (with or without a partner). No need to wonder why: sex is hardwired into us. It's one of our most basic survival mechanisms, and it makes us feel good. Really good. As good as a jolt of heroin, in fact.

Orgasm is the most powerful legal high you can get anywhere, igniting the same pleasure centers in the brain that get turned on by cocaine, heroin, and other addictive drugs.

The urge for that high can be so powerful that when we're blindsided by desire, it's often difficult to figure out what's happening in our body, let alone our brain. Sometimes it seems our brains aren't involved at all when it comes to sex—that we've been hijacked by our genitals.

But the fact is that your brain, not your body, calls the shots (literally). The true sex organ is between your ears.

Your Brain on Sex

Desire starts with a thought, a scent, a touch, or the sight of an object of desire, and this is as true for women as it is for men. But scientists still haven't figured out everything that happens in the brain between that first tweak and orgasm. However, thanks to new imaging techniques and cooperative subjects willing to have sex under observation, they're collecting a lot of sometimes surprising information about what goes on in your brain on sex. They're finding that the arousal-to-orgasm trip winds through many parts of your brain, that men and women tend to be turned on by a lot of the same things, and that the brains of homosexuals are more like their preferred sex partners than their biological gender.

They're also finding that some brain parts have to get turned off for us to get really turned on. Orgasm requires a release of inhibitions, a shutdown of the brain's center of vigilance in both sexes, and what looks like a widespread neural power failure in females. The fight-or-flight sentry center in the amygdala seems to swoon when either sex has an orgasm. And the pleasure centers tend to light up brightly in the brain scans of both sexes, especially in those of males.

Neuroscientist Gert Holstege of the University of Groningen in the Netherlands and his colleagues discovered these brain actions while scanning men and women reaching orgasm. They had female partners of eleven men stimulate their partner's penis until he ejaculated while they scanned his brain using positron emission tomography (PET). During ejaculation, activity in the men's amygdala declined, while there was extraordinarily intense activation in a major hub of the brain's reward circuitry, the ventral tegmental area. Brain regions involved in memory-related imagery and in vision also turned on, and the anterior part of the cerebellum, which is involved in emotional processing, switched into high gear.

The team then used PET scans to see what orgasm looked like in the brains of twelve women while their partner stimulated their clitoris to climax. When she reached orgasm, brain activity fell in her amygdala too. But something unexpected happened: much of her brain went silent. Some of the most muted neurons sat in the left lateral orbitofrontal cortex, which may govern self-control over basic desires such as sex. Decreased activity there, the researchers suggest, might correspond to a release of tension and inhibition. The scientists also saw

LOVE POTION NO. 9: IT'S A CHEMICAL KIND OF THING

Sexual delight comes from a cascade of pleasure-producing hormones and neurotransmitters that tickle our reward center, setting off a rainbow rush of good feelings and, perhaps, a desire to stay together.

Dopamine, the neurochemical of all addictions and desires, sets off the reward system by triggering the release of testosterone, the hormone that drives the libido in both men and women and surges in orgasm. The hormone prolactin gives sexual gratification and helps lower the arousal effects of dopamine, opening the door for arginine vasopressin, which is associated with pair bonding, as is oxytocin, perhaps the true love potion. The neurohormone of mother love, trust, and bonding, it's called the "cuddle hormone" because it promotes that postclimax loving feeling, but it's different in men than it is in women. In women, estrogen enhances the oxytocin loving effects, while in men, testosterone tends to offset some oxytocin effects.

a dip in excitation in the dorsomedial prefrontal cortex, which has an apparent role in moral reasoning and social judgment—a change that may be tied to a suspension of judgment and reflection (and explain why smart women can make dumb choices in men).

But in another study of women and orgasm, the brains told a different story. Brain activation was imaged during orgasm in five women with spinal cord injuries that left them without sensation in their lower extremities. These women reached "deep," or nonclitoral, orgasm through mechanical stimulation (using a laboratory device) of the vagina and cervix. But contrary to Holstege's results, this team found that orgasm was accompanied by a general activation of the limbic system, the brain's seat of emotion—including the amygdala. Also activated was the hypothalamus, which produces oxytocin, the putative love and bonding hormone whose levels jump fourfold at orgasm. The researchers also found heightened activity in the nucleus accumbens, a critical part of the brain's reward circuit, and in the anterior cingulate cortex and the insula, two brain areas some researchers have found associated with the later stages of love relationships.

Women, Men, and Orgasms: How Alike Are They?

The need for male orgasm is obvious: sperm has to be produced and ejaculated to meet up with an egg and make a replacement *you*. But scientists are still stymied about what survival role orgasm plays for women. It might retain sperm, increasing chances of conception. Or it may increase bonding with a mate, and so involve more complex thoughts and feelings in women than it does in men.

Researchers are trying to crack this riddle by probing brain activity during arousal and orgasm, and they are finding many similarities between the sexes in various sexual functions. Preliminary evidence suggests that the central control of sexual functions in men and women is remarkably similar. The same neurochemicals fuel the flames of desire, and the same brain parts light up under imaging scans. Women also have nocturnal "erections" (a swelling arousal of the labia, vagina, and clitoris) four or five times a night during REM sleep. Like their male counterparts, women who are paraplegics can experience orgasm.

The so-called higher brain centers get involved in both genders, but we know less about how this happens. PET studies show that parts of the cerebral cortex associated with emotional experiences are activated when men are aroused, and its functions of memory and desire can direct erections. Women may have better orgasms when they are in love (see "What's Love Got to Do with It?" page 153). And both genders are vulnerable to sexual dysfunction when taking some medications, including antidepressants.

Of course, there are also dramatic differences. There is a delay between orgasms for men, and the ability to get and sustain an erection weakens with age. Women can have multiple orgasms, and sexual arousal and function do not fade with time.

Women also appear to be more fluid about sex. In a 2008 American Psychological Association longitudinal study of female bisexuality that studied seventy-nine women over a ten-year period, researchers found no evidence for the commonly held view that bisexuality is an experimental phase en route to lesbianism or heterosexuality. They found that bisexuality in women is a distinct and consistent sexual orientation. They also found that as women age, they tend to turn more toward bisexuality and become more likely than heterosexuals or lesbians to settle into monogamous relationships.

Does the Penis Have a Brain of Its Own?

It certainly seems so at times. It may insist on attention in inconvenient circumstances or refuse to participate when its owner asks. So in a way, the answer to the question is yes, though one can't really call it a brain. It's more of an erection-generating reflex that responds to nerve signals created by physical stimulation. It appears that the penis and its purposes are so vital to the survival of our species that there are backups and safeguards to protect reproductive function if something goes wrong in the brain.

The penis and brain do stay in contact, sending each other messages along the spinal cord where they influence nerve pathways. But the penis can function very well without the brain. Men can have erections and ejaculations without involvement of the brain function. It's common for men to awake with an erection without any stimulation or even sexy dream.

An erection does not even require an intact spinal cord, as researchers have discovered from men who have damaged or even severed spinal cords and still father children. In fact, when the brain is disconnected from the penis, erections are more frequent.

It seems there is an erection-generating section—a kind of penis brain—located in the sacral segments of the spinal cord, just above the tailbone in men. Physical stimulation of the penis sends sensory signals to this erection center, which activates a cascade of messages to tell the penile blood vessels its time to boot up.

An erect penis appears to be the default state. One of the important functions of the brain is to suppress erections most of the time, so that men can go about other business and also protect the blood vessels from damage from being constantly engorged. When a man is not sexually aroused, parts of the sympathetic nervous system actively limit blood flow to the penis, keeping it limp. Viagra—also known as sildenafil—works by slowing the breakdown of one of the chemicals that keeps the muscles relaxed, holding blood in the penis.

Studies have also shown that men can learn to have erections on demand using only their brains, in response to mental imagery or non-sexual cues or through the use of imagery and fantasy. This explains why an astounding number of fetish objects, such as high-heeled shoes, leather whips, and flimsy lingerie, can be a turn-on.

Higher brain centers are involved in male erections as well, particularly learning and memory, but we know much less about them.

It isn't just men who get turned on by erotic images: sexual images with no emotional connection arouse women as well. And it seems that women are turned on by more varied sex options than men are, says psychologist Meredith Chivers of the Center for Addiction and Mental Health in Toronto. In her study, about a hundred homosexual and heterosexual men and women were monitored while watching erotic film

---

A KISS IS MORE THAN JUST A KISS

Wonder why some of us like kissing on the lips? Although it's not universal in all cultures, some scientists theorize that kissing can be a major exchange of information and a crucial part of mate selection.

A kiss is the catalyst for a flood of neural messages and chemicals that transmit tactile sensations, sexual excitement, feelings of closeness, motivation, and even euphoria. Because your lips are densely populated with sensory neurons, the touch goes right to your head (literally). And the olfactory information from kissing may also play a role in mate selection, helping us discover genetic material to complement our own.

clips that included same-sex intercourse, solitary masturbation, nude exercise performed by men and women, male-female intercourse, and mating between bonobos (close ape relatives of the chimpanzee). Whereas men tended to be turned on by images of their preferred gender of sexual partner (gay or straight), heterosexual women's level of arousal increased along with the intensity of the sexual activity no matter who or what was engaged in it. In fact, these women were genitally excited by male and female actors equally and also responded to images of bonobo apes having sex.

What's Love Got to Do with It? Plenty, It Turns Out— for Women

Women can certainly have orgasms without love. Nevertheless, research backs up the obvious: a woman in love has better orgasms, suggesting that the feelings a woman has for her sexual partner are tied to just how good her orgasms are.

Researchers at Geneva University in Switzerland and the University of California, Santa Barbara, asked twenty-nine head-over-heels heterosexual women to rate the intensity of their love as well as the quality, ease, and frequency of orgasms with their partner. Then they mapped brain activity with functional magnetic resonance imaging (fMRI) while the women focused on an unrelated thinking task. As the women worked, their lover's name flashed on screens in front of them too quickly to be noticed consciously but slowly enough to evoke a subliminal response from the brain—a technique that has been shown to reveal the neural networks involved in partner recognition and related emotions.

The more "in love" the subjects reported being, the greater activity the name flash triggered in the left angular gyrus, a brain region involved in memories of events and emotions. The most smitten subjects also reported having orgasms more easily—and far better ones too—with ease and quality linked to a region involved in reward and addiction.

"The more they were satisfied by their sexual relationship in terms of orgasm, the more this brain area was activated," says psychologist and study coauthor Stephanie Ortigue. However, there was no link between intensity of love and how often the women climaxed.

Are You Born Gay? Sexual Orientation Is Biology, Not Choice

Many gay men and lesbians say they knew they preferred the same sex from the time they were children. Research is showing that's probably true, as more evidence accumulates that sexual orientation is neither a choice nor something in the way people are brought up. It's something that people are born with.

In a recent study, brain scans show that the brains of gay men are similar to those of straight women—and that the brains of heterosexual men and lesbians are similar. The brain characteristics they scanned develop in the womb or in early infancy, meaning that psychological or environmental factors played little or no role, said researchers at the Stockholm Brain Institute in Sweden.

The researchers used magnetic resonance imaging scans to look at the brains of ninety volunteers: twenty-five straight and twenty gay members of each sex. They found that the straight men and gay women had asymmetrical brains; that is, the cerebrum was larger on the right hemisphere of the brain than on the left. But the brains of straight women and gay men had symmetrical cerebrums.

The team next used PET scans to measure the blood flow to the amygdala, the seat of emotion, fear, and aggression. To minimize external and learned influences, they scanned the brains when at rest and did not show the participants photos or introduce any behavior that might have been learned. Here they found that in gay men and straight women, the blood flowed to areas involved in fear and anxiety—but in straight men and lesbians, it tended to flow to pockets linked to aggression.

The question about whether sex partner preference is genetic is still unresolved. And if genes are involved, do they create two distinct types of orientation—gay and straight, as most people believe? And where does bisexuality fit in?

Although no one study is entirely conclusive, studies of twins raised together, twins raised apart, and family trees suggest—at least for males—that the more genes you share with a homosexual relative, the more likely you are to be homosexual.

But no advances in science will ever completely resolve the moral and philosophical issues around sexual orientation, say those who study human sexuality. Enormous pressures push most of us toward a heterosexual orientation from the time we are very young. Also, some religious and other groups claim gays can switch to straight if they really want to. While that's true for some, experts say most gays cannot, and even if they do, they are not comfortable about it.

11 p.m.

Falling Asleep

Your eyelids are getting heavy, very heavy, and so is this book on your lap. You are, in a word, hypnagogic: drifting in the drowsy transitional stage that comes right before nodding off.

Adenosine, a chemical of sleepiness, has been building up in your body all day long, making you sleepy, very sleepy. Now your inner body clock has flipped the switch to your pituitary, and melatonin, the hormone of darkness, is seeping through your brain. Soon your mind and body will enter the restful rhythmic stages of unconsciousness.

Until a few decades ago, not much was known about the brain during sleep. Sleep was thought to be a passive state during which nothing much happened except for those pesky dreams, which, Freud and Jung told us, were signs our unconscious mind was trying to tell us something. (See "Midnight.") Then imaging and experiments showed sleep to be quite an active process, during which our brain doesn't take much rest at all. Scientists still don't know why we sleep, but they know it's vital for health.

The Five Stages of Sleep

While we're sleeping, body, mind, and brain typically pass through five distinct stages that repeat and cycle all night long every 90 to 110 minutes, or between four and five times per night.

Stage 1 is a light sleep when we drift close to consciousness and can be easily awakened. In stage 2, where adults spend half of their sleep time, brain waves slow down and eye movements stop. Deep sleep takes over in stages 3 and 4. In stage 3, the electrical activity in your brain slows: very slow brain activity called delta waves appear, and by stage 4, they predominate. It's very hard to awaken someone in deep sleep, and this is the sleep stage when some people, especially young children, sleepwalk. (See "2:00 A.M.")

During these stages, most neurons in the brain stem above the spinal cord appear to slow or stop firing, and breathing and heart rate settle into regular rhythms. But most neurons in the cerebral cortex

---

HOW LONG CAN SOMEONE STAY AWAKE?

The quick answer is 264 hours, or eleven days. In 1965 Randy Gardner, a seventeen-year-old high school student, set this apparent world record as a science fair project.

Several other research subjects have remained awake for eight to ten days in carefully monitored experiments. All showed progressive and significant losses in concentration, motivation, perception, and other higher mental processes, but none had serious problems, and all returned to relative normalcy after one or two nights of sleep. There are reports of soldiers staying awake for four days in battle and patients with mania going without sleep for three to four days. And some rare medical conditions can keep people awake for weeks.

But the more complete answer revolves around the definition of the word *awake.* In prolonged sleep deprivation in normal people, there are numerous brief episodes of light sleep (lasting a few seconds), often described as microsleep, alternating with drowsy wakefulness, as well as loss of thinking and motor functions. Many of us know about the accidents caused by the dangerous drowsy driver who falls asleep for a few seconds. Gardner was "awake," but basically he was cognitively dysfunctional by the end of his ordeal.

HOW MUCH SLEEP DO WE NEED?

Sleep experts say most of us aren't getting enough sleep. Here's what the National Sleep Foundation says we need. But keep in mind that your sleep needs are as individual as you, your genetics, and your lifestyle. And a timely nap may mean less nighttime sleep need.

- Babies take the sleep they need: sixteen to eighteen hours out of twenty-four, more or less.
- Toddlers sleep about fifteen hours, young children eleven to thirteen hours.
- School-age kids need ten to eleven hours.
- Teens need nine or more sleep hours but seldom get it. They would need to sleep past 8:00 A.M., which is starting time (or after starting time) for many U.S. schools and has prompted some high schools to begin and end later in the day.
- Adults need eight hours but generally get just around seven.
- Elders sleep a bit more but have more trouble getting asleep and staying asleep. They may also break up sleep into shorter segments, day and night, and so they think they are sleeping less.

And by the way, small animals require much more sleep than large animals, with opossums craving eighteen hours and elephants only three hours a day.

and adjacent forebrain regions slow activity only a little bit. They begin firing in synchronicity with a relatively low-frequency rhythm, rather like an idling car engine. This is when some basic cell repair seems to take place.

During stage 5, or rapid eye movement (REM) sleep, neurons are much more active—almost as active in your brain as when you are awake. Most neurons in the forebrain and the brain stem communicate with other neurons at rates as high as or even higher than the awake brain, and they use as much energy. This is the stage where we dream and when men (and women) may have erections. The sympathetic nervous system relaxes, allowing blood to flow to the genitals. While you are in these deepest stages of sleep, commands from your brain to your muscles are suppressed by the chemical messenger gamma-aminobutyric acid so that your limbs are temporarily paralyzed.

Meanwhile, your breathing, blood pressure, and heart rate accelerate, and your eyes jerk rapidly (which is what gives this stage of sleep its name). We spend about 20 percent of our sleep time in REM, with the REM session getting longer each time, and the last one is usually right before we awake. REM sessions begin to decrease in length as we age, by the way.

Insomnia: Curse of the Night

You've been tossing for half an hour or more, and those five stages of sleep are but a dream. Or maybe a nightmare. Having trouble putting mind and body to rest? It's a curse for millions, who dread facing bedtime. Some 30 percent of the population reports trouble falling asleep or staying asleep as a chronic, and not just a sometimes, thing.

If you are sleepless in Seattle, or anywhere else, there could be a health reason. When the tossing-turning aggravation of sleeplessness sets in, most of us are quick to blame an overactive mind or emotions. But it could be wise to look first to the body, not the brain. Common physical reasons for sleeplessness are sleep apnea, medications or their interactions, caffeine (it's in chocolate as well as coffee and tea), restless leg syndrome, and stress and pain.

When these problems are taken care of, sleepless bouts usually get better on their own. But for too many people, these sleep problems turn into insomnia, a not-so-benign condition that not only can affect your social life but raises the risk of depression, obesity, heart disease, and diabetes.

Sleep experts are looking at some new evidence that reverses older thinking. Many insomniacs believe that they don't get enough sleep.

But research is showing that they are in fact getting at least as much as they need, and possibly more. That's because insomniacs tend to go to bed early, stay there late, and sleep during the day—all of which contribute to the problem.

Researchers are also finding that your opinions about sleep affect the kind of sleep you'll have. Insomniacs are more likely to be concerned about not sleeping and to think about problems, events of the day, and noises in the environment while preparing to sleep. They also underestimate the amount of time they actually sleep and how much sleep they need

Although eight hours a night is a figure repeated so often that it has almost become an article of faith, the reality is that sleep need is highly individual. But if you believe you need eight hours of sleep a night, you will arrange your schedule so that you spend eight hours in bed. If you need only six hours of sleep, however, you'll spend two hours of those hours tossing and turning.

Perhaps Less Is More?

Large-scale epidemiological studies have shown that sleeping seven hours a night is associated with the lowest mortality risk (for many conditions such as heart disease, cancer, and accidental death) compared with longer or shorter periods of shut-eye. Also, the longer you're awake, the more slow-wave (delta) sleep you'll have (slow-wave sleep is what leads to feeling rested and refreshed).

Many people believe that if they have a good night's sleep, they will wake up without an alarm, feeling rested and refreshed. Yet circadian rhythm studies show that people are usually drowsy early in the morning even after a full night's sleep. If you are truly sleep deprived, you will have trouble remaining awake during the day.

There are plenty of nondrug treatments for insomnia, most of them based on common sense. If insomnia remains a problem, though, you might want to see your doctor for more help.

And maybe it's not really insomnia.

Interrupted Sleep? Don't Call It Insomnia.
It's Normal

Do you wake up after a few hours of sleep and find yourself wide-eyed for an hour or two before dropping off again? Research from several sources suggests this segmented sleep is actually normal sleep and was common until modern times.

The assault on the eight-hour consolidated sleep belief comes from sleep researchers and an unexpected historical source. In his book *At Day's Close: Night in Times Past,* history professor Roger Ekirch reveals that in preindustrial times before artificial lights, people would go to bed with the sun, wake after a few hours, and then fall back asleep at 2:00 A.M. or so until dawn. This period between first and second sleep was spent in quiet contemplation, doing household chores, visiting, and sexual intimacy. It also afforded a time to contemplate (and discuss) first-sleep dreams.

Quite coincidentally, some sleep researchers have been reaching similar conclusions. They have found that breaking a night's sleep into two sections may be more in tune with our circadian rhythms and the natural environment. It seems this two-sleep pattern is embedded in mammalian evolution: many mammals sleep in two shifts, just as we used to do, says sleep researcher Thomas A. Wehr.

IS SLEEP LIKE A COMA?

Nope. Though people under anesthesia or in a coma are often said to "be asleep," they can't be awakened and don't produce the complex, active brain wave patterns seen in normal sleep. Instead, their brain waves are very slow and weak, sometimes all but undetectable.

Remember that reticular activating system (RAS) that helped wake you at 5:00 A.M.? Many general anesthetics work to quiet this part of your brain, and damage to your RAS can cause coma.

So it seems, actually, that a good eight hours may be two four-hour sleep sessions. The current seven to eight hours of uninterrupted sleep may be a product of today's artificially illuminated nights and a result of chronic sleep deprivation, Wehr says. Another sleep researcher, Todd Arnedt, speculates that if people were told interrupted sleep was perfectly normal, they might be less worried and thus fall back asleep more easily.

So if you find yourself awake in the middle of the night, don't despair. Take this found time to read, meditate, take a warm bath, or have sex with a similarly awakened partner. For you, two-step sleep may be perfectly normal.

Call Me Sleepless

Many of us enjoy an occasional bedtime chat with a loved one who is far away. Alas, if you make that late-night call with a mobile phone, you may find insomnia has your number and is speed-dialing it.

Studies are showing that cell phone signals can alter brain waves, and that might keep you up at night. Neuroscientist Rodney Croft and his colleagues at Swinburne University of Technology in Australia strapped a Nokia 6110 cell phone to the heads of 120 men and women and then monitored their brain waves. When the researchers switched on the phone (without telling the subjects), they saw a sudden power boost in the volunteers' alpha brain waves. Croft believes the heightened alpha waves reflect the mind as it concentrates to overcome the electrical interference in brain circuits caused by the pulsed microwave radiation from cell phones.

In a different study, sleep researchers at Loughborough University in England found that after a thirty-minute exposure to cell phone signals in talk mode, people took nearly twice as long to fall asleep as they did when the phone had been off or in standby mode. The scientists think the effect probably reflects the time it takes the brain to relax after being agitated by the phone's electrical field. James Horne, a renowned sleep expert and one of the study's authors, cautions that the effects are harmless and less disruptive to sleep than drinking a half-cup of coffee. Still, he wonders, "With different doses, durations or other devices, would there be greater effects?"

Still Awake? Can You Catch Up on Lost Sleep?

While sleep is eluding you, let's do some sleep math. You lost two hours of sleep every night last week because of a big project due on Friday. On the weekend you slept in, getting four extra hours. Come Monday morning, you were feeling bright-eyed. But don't be duped by your apparent vim and vigor: you're still carrying around a heavy load of what experts call "sleep debt"—in this case, almost a full night's sleep.

Sleep debt—the difference between the amount of sleep you should be getting and the amount you actually get—grows every time we skim some extra minutes off nightly slumber. Studies show this short-term sleep deprivation leads to a foggy brain, worsened vision, impaired driving, and trouble remembering. Long-term effects include obesity, insulin resistance, and heart disease.

The good news is that like all other debt, sleep debt can be repaid—though it won't happen in one extended snooze marathon. The chronically sleep deprived take a few months to get back into a natural sleep pattern, says Lawrence J. Epstein, medical director of the Harvard-affiliated Sleep Health Centers.

Tacking on an extra hour or two of sleep a night is the way to catch up. Go to bed when you are tired, and allow your body to wake you in the morning (no alarm clock allowed). You may find yourself catatonic in the beginning of the recovery cycle. Expect to bank upward of ten hours shut-eye per night.

As the days pass and you erase sleep debt, your body will come to rest at a sleep pattern that is specifically right for you. Sleep researchers believe that our genes determine our individual sleeping patterns. (See "Are You a Lark or an Owl?" in "5:00 A.M.") So follow the dictates of your innate sleep needs. You'll feel better.

Is Insomnia Worse for Night Owls?

Early to bed, early to rise may be wise after all. It seems that late-to-bed, late-to-rise insomniacs have more emotional distress than early risers despite actually getting more sleep.

Researchers questioned 312 insomniacs who went to the Stanford (University) Sleep Disorders Clinic for group therapy and categorized them as a morning or evening person or an intermediate. They found night owls went to bed an hour or more later than morning and intermediate types, but reported more time spent sleeping and more time in bed. On average, they slept 6.4 hours, compared with 5.9 for early risers, and spent 8.7 hours in bed compared with 7.9.

Even after data were adjusted for the amount of time they spent awake in bed, there were still differences between the night owls and the morning people, says Jason Ong, a behavioral sleep psychologist at Stanford University and lead author of the report. For one thing, night owls were less consistent in when they went to bed and got up. And they seemed to hold more negative and more rigid beliefs about what their sleep should be, Ong says. Night owls reported feeling less in control of their sleep and feeling that they have a hard time getting through the day with less sleep, which might perpetuate insomnia, the researchers say. And they had more risk factors for depression.

12 *midnight*

Sleeping in the Midnight Hour

Your mind, body, and brain are unconscious, sinking into the deep sleep of stages 3 and 4. Your whole self is on idle, and very slow delta waves predominate in your brain. It would be hard to wake you now, and if you are awakened, you'll be groggy and disoriented.

These are the nourishing sleep stages when growth hormones are released, cells are repaired and discarded, and, scientists think, learning consolidated. (See "1:00 A.M.")

Strolling in Your Sleep

But not all of us are at rest. When in the throes of deep sleep, some of us may behave as though we are awake from time to time. Young children whose brains may not be able to resist movement are especially likely to sleepwalk, have night terrors, or wet the bed.

Sleepwalking happens only during the non–rapid-eye-movement cycle of deep sleep. It's due to a mix-up in brain messages. While you are in these deepest stages of sleep, commands from your brain to your muscles are suppressed by the chemical messenger gamma-aminobutyric acid (GABA). This keeps you from making unconscious movements and possible injuring yourself (or others sharing your bed).

But when this brake is off, people have done just about everything in deep sleep, from walking and talking to housecleaning, and even driving a car. If awakened, they're often confused and unaware they've been up and about.

This neurochemical error is more common during childhood, perhaps because children spend more time in this deep sleep phase and possibly because they lack enough GABA neurotransmitter. The neurons that release GABA are still developing in young children. If they don't have enough GABA, their motor neurons can command the body to move even during sleep, says Antonio Oliviero of the National Hospital for Paraplegics in Toledo, Spain.

Adults may sleepwalk because their GABA system didn't develop properly. It could be genetics: sleepwalking runs in families, and the identical twin of a person who sleepwalks typically does so as well. Your deep sleep could also be sabotaged by environmental factors. Studies have shown that frequent sleepwalking is associated with sleep deprivation, fever, stress, and drugs, especially sedatives, hypnotics, antipsychotics, stimulants, antihistamines, and sleep drugs: there are reports of people sleep-eating, sleep-driving, and more while taking a popular insomnia drug.

The best way to respond to sleepwalking? Lead wandering people gently back to bed and tuck them in. Chances are sleepwalkers won't remember a thing in the morning.

Drifting into Dreamland

Right about 12:30 A.M., if you slipped into sleep at around 11:00 P.M., your brain is about to enter the dream zone of REM sleep that follows ninety minutes or so of slow wave sleep.

You may have had some dreamlike mini-moments in that hypnogogic state before falling asleep and when just awakening, when fragmented images or mini-dramas flashed ever so briefly across your fading consciousness. That's normal, and probably what people are referring to when they speak of "lucid dreaming."

But dreams mainly take place in the REM stage of sleep, which will repeat every 90 to 110 minutes and last for 10 minutes or more, gradually increasing in length until you awake. Scientists think everyone dreams during REM—even those of us who claim not to. We don't know for sure if babies dream, but they spend a lot of time in REM sleep. Even in utero, babies are in REM sleep 10 of 24 hours.

During REM sleep, your limbs are paralyzed for your own safety. But your heart rate and breathing become irregular, as they are when you are awake, and your emotional and memory areas—your amygdala and hippocampus—are very active.

And we dream.

Dreams have long intrigued us. Are they portents of the future, a replaying of the past, or the surfacing of hidden desires? Are they the brain's way of resolving issues, or of dumping mental and emotional garbage? These questions go back to antiquity. Scientists still don't have an answer, but they have plenty of theories.

Sigmund Freud believed dreaming was "the royal road" to the unconscious—a direct pipeline into our disguised and deepest thoughts, desires, and feelings. He believed dreams revealed our repressed wishes. Research hasn't shown that to be true, and for a while, neuroscientists were arguing that dreams were just the result of meaningless neuronal activity.

They know dreams are the by-products of neurological processes associated with sleep and that they're usually linked with REM sleep, which is governed by the pons, a part of the brainstem involved in arousal. So one theory is that an overactive pons generates random images and information based on stored memories or random bursts of electrical brain activity.

More currently, scientists are finding that dreams may be the result, if not the content, of our busy brain's activity during REM sleep. Indeed, research shows the brain is almost as active during REM as when we're awake.

Some research suggests dreams help your brain edit and file experiences. Studies show we consolidate and reprocess newly learned information into memory during REM sleep, which could explain why we often dream about recent experiences. REM seems to be especially important for reinforcing new motor activities. Rats, for

WILL YOU DIE WITHOUT REM SLEEP?

There's a myth that we die if we don't dream. It seems to be true for lab rats (the four-legged kind). Although no one knows the cause of death, rats robbed of REM for four weeks die.

But this hasn't been shown in any species other than rats, says psychiatrist Jerry Siegel, head of the Center for Sleep Research at the University of California, Los Angeles. "Dying from lack of REM is totally bogus," Siegel says. He recently proved that REM is nonexistent in some big-brained mammals, such as dolphins and whales.

Many people don't dream and don't die as a result. When humans take some types of antidepressants, their dreams disappear along with REM sleep, and millions are on antidepressants and still alive. Also, patients with brain damage who don't experience REM don't seem to suffer from dream loss.

example, run through mazes in their dreams that precisely match their real-life lab mazes, so it's likely there's some purpose or meaningful information in dreams.

A related theory suggests that the function of dreams is to delete unnecessary memories, clearing the brain of its excess baggage—sort of like running defrag on your computer. And some experts believe that dreams are a primitive form of thinking associated with subconscious or even psychotic thought.

Studies show that sleep can help us solve problems and reach new insights. So it's possible your mind is busily sorting through the treasures and trash of your thoughts to make meaningful movies in your brain. But so far, science is showing this to be more a property of brain chemistry and recent memories than an outbreak of disguised desires.

Perhaps, suggests one scientist, we need to understand thought before we can understand dreaming. Although much about dreams remains unresolved, we do know that dreams are as unique as we are, related to our own situations and individuality.

Indeed, our dreams undoubtedly have some emotional messages—just not perhaps for the reasons, or in the ways, Freud envisioned them.

Do Banished Thoughts Resurface in Dreams?

Sigmund Freud thought so. Nobody knows yet, but a study of 330 dreaming college students suggests that in this case, he may be right. Harvard University psychologist Daniel M. Wegner and his colleagues asked the students to think of an acquaintance and then spend five minutes in one of three mental exercises before going to sleep. The first group focused their thoughts on the person, the second group suppressed thoughts about the person, and the third group could think about anything that came to mind.

In the morning when they wrote down their dreams, researchers found that students focused on a specific person dreamed about them more than those who could think about anything. But they also found the group that made a conscious effort to block someone from their minds dreamed of them the most.

One explanation is that unwelcome thoughts might resurface in dreams because the prefrontal cortex is less active, so the brain is less able to keep them at bay. But these could also be, as Freud said, indicators of what we try not to think of during the day, Wegner suggests.

Want to Dream More? Try Sleep Deprivation

Your brain likes REM. It's almost is if the brain is keeping score: miss a few dreams from lack of sleep, and your brain will make the next ones more intense. Sometimes nightmare intense.

The phenomenon is called REM rebound, and it's been confirmed through sleep deprivation studies in which researchers awaken subjects as they enter REM sleep. After a few awakenings, the urge for REM increases to where they jump immediately to REM as soon as they fall asleep, bypassing the usual sleep stages.

In a study published in the journal *Sleep,* Tore Nielsen, director of the Dream and Nightmare Lab at the Sacré-Coeur Hospital in Montreal, showed that losing thirty minutes of REM one night can lead to a 35 percent REM increase the next night: a jump from seventy-four minutes of REM to a rebound total of a hundred minutes. Nielsen also found that dream intensity increased with REM deprivation. Those who were getting only about twenty-five minutes of REM sleep rated the quality of their dreams between 9 and 8 on a 9-point scale (1 being dull, 9 being dynamite).

Most of us aren't strangers to REM deprivation and rebound. Alcohol and nicotine both repress REM, as do blood pressure drugs and antidepressants. So if you don't want to wrestle alligators or delight in fantasies in your sleep, aim for more regular shut-eye hours—and less drinking and smoking.

Part 6

NIGHT CREW AT WORK
1 A.M. TO 4 A.M.

Night Crew at Work

While you are sleeping, your body and mind are on vacation. Consciousness is lolling somewhere in a metaphoric hammock, muscles are taking a rest, vision is out for the night, and the dial is turned down, way down, on hearing, body temperature, respiration, and heart rate.

But your brain is up and about, like a fussy host tidying up after the guests have gone. Your brain will stay busy all night long with housekeeping chores: strengthening memories and some neural connections, lopping off unneeded cells and synaptic connections, releasing growth hormone, and taking a break every ninety minutes or so for dreaming. If you can call that a break.

Dreaming, of course, occupies our REM sleep. And some essential repair work seems to get under way during non-REM deep sleep: many cells up their production, including proteins, and your immune system gets recharged.

Your brain also uses this downtime to downsize, as it discards little-used neural pathways and strengthens others. Think of it as roadwork: the busy streets get repaved and improved for easier travel, the little-used byways get ignored and then abandoned. Pruning (a term that scientists actually use) is a good analogy. As gardeners know, cutting back weak or useless parts strengthens the whole plant. Some researchers argue that this synaptic downsizing is one of the main functions of sleep, thus allowing your brain to make new connections when you awake.

Other research shows that your brain takes advantage of sleep to sift through and process the information it has been acquiring all day long. It files and copies memories, discards others, makes connections among newly acquired data, practices skills it learned while you were awake, and even solves problems and helps you reach decisions. All while you sleep.

This information about your brain's twenty-four-hour workday is relatively new. Until the mid-twentieth century, it was pretty much taken for granted that sleep turned off the brain as well as the mind and body, and that not much happened while you snoozed. Then scientists discovered that the brain produces waves—oscillating electromagnetic signals—during sleep phases, and that those produced during the REM phase looked very much like the brain waves in an awake and active brain. Further research showed your brain is active during all phases of sleep, using that time to take itself into the shop for repairs and upgrades.

A sleeping brain is not merely on standby. It runs through a suite of complex and orderly activities. There's a flow of activity from neurons in the hippocampus (where short-term memories are formed) to the cortex, where they are stored in more durable forms—a possible reason people can remember things better upon awakening.

The night crew is hard at work.

Cleaning Up Your Neural Garbage

Housekeeping in your brain is more than a metaphor. Studies are showing your body is constantly at work to vacuum up cellular debris that could gum up the works. Indeed, researchers are now wondering if dementia could be the result of bad housekeeping in your brain.

Every day and night, your body removes damaged and dying cells in a process called autophagy (or "self-eating," from the Greek), much the way our bodies dispose of invading viruses and bacteria. Autophagosomes clean up and digest the cytoplasm inside your cells, where a vast and intricate array of complex operations produces—basically—trash. Proteins, for instance, which carry out all the work of the cell, are sometimes put together wrong and can stop functioning or, worse, may malfunction. Autophagy cleans up the cytoplasm that's clotted with old bits of protein and other unwanted sludge made up of old and damaged cellular machinery.

It could be that taking out the neural trash plays a role in determining your life span, keeping your vital cells healthier and stronger longer. A good cleaning is particularly important to neurons, because they are long-lived—as long-lived as you, in most cases.

Slovenly autophagy might play a pivotal role in some neurodegenerative disorders such as Alzheimer's, Parkinson's, and Huntington's diseases. All of these brain diseases are characterized by clumps of defective proteins and other cellular trash that the cells fail to clear away. Some think this is evidence that autophagy is failing to do its job.

Your cells may decide all by themselves (or be instructed by other cells) to make the ultimate sacrifice, with controlled cellular suicide, called apoptosis. Your cells carry a death program, like a spy who has a cyanide pill in a hollowed tooth, ready to self-destruct when necessary for the good of the whole organism. A damaged or aging cell that no longer functions may bite the bullet. Indeed, inducing a controlled apoptosis might be a treatment for cancerous cells that grow out of control.

Why Your Brain Doesn't Take a Break Already

Exactly why your brain works the night shift isn't known, but researchers have some theories. Sleep and cognition experts Robert Stickgold and Jeffrey M. Ellenbogen of Harvard Medical School suggest it might be that your brain takes advantage of the ancient evolutionary pressures to hunt during daylight and rest in the dark. Since the brain was already set up to sleep, it makes sense it evolved further to acquire information by day and process it by night.

Or, they suggest, it might be the reverse. Processing memories seems to require us to stop dealing with our surroundings and incoming signals. Of all the functions of sleep, memory processing is the only one that explains why you'd have to go through the dangerous phenomenon of losing consciousness as opposed to having quiet rest, says Stickgold.

Some experts believe sleep also helps detoxify the brain. The lower metabolic rate and brain temperature during non-REM sleep could benefit that housekeeping process.

What most experts do agree is that sleep is necessary and good—and that most of us could use a bit more of it. (See "2:00 A.M.")

STIMULATING THE SLEEPING BRAIN MIGHT BOOST MEMORY

Studies show your brain can better consolidate memories of just-learned facts when you "sleep on it." It appears that a little externally applied electricity on your sleeping brain might boost memory even better.

Memory consolidation is suspected to take place during slow-wave (or delta wave) sleep. But although the brain generates oscillating waves of neuronal activity during this phase, these brain waves weren't considered important to the process.

Jan Born and colleagues at the University of Lübeck in Germany gave a simple memory test involving sets of word pairs to thirteen volunteer medical students and then let them fall asleep. As expected, their ability to remember the words improved after a nap.

Born's team then put electrodes on the volunteers' heads, and as they dozed off and were about to enter slow-wave sleep, the scientists induced a slowly oscillating current slightly stronger than the brain's natural one. They spaced five sessions of this stimulation over half an hour, and when volunteers awoke, they could remember almost three more word pairs than control subjects who were given sham treatment.

Perhaps enhancing the brain wave patterns in other sleep stages might boost other types of memory. Memories of skills, for example, are consolidated during the later stage of REM sleep when your brain's electrical activity is dominated by the higher-frequency theta wave.

The 10 Percent Myth

By now you can see the fallacy of the old myth that we use only 10 percent of our brains. This misconception is among the most deeply entrenched in all of popular psychology. It has contributed to a plethora of self-help books and self-improvement gadgets, including devices that supposedly enable us to harness our unrealized capacities.

The seductive appeal is understandable: we'd love to believe that our brain harbors an enormous reservoir of untapped potential. But scientific evidence, especially functional magnetic resonance imaging (fMRI) studies, has consistently failed to turn up any region of the brain that is perpetually inactive.

The 10 percent myth probably stems in part from a misinterpretation of the writings of William James, one of the founders of American psychology. In his musings around the turn of the twentieth century, James wrote that most of us actualize only a small portion of our intellectual potential, an assertion that may well possess some merit. But several popular authors, including Lowell Thomas, who penned the foreword to Dale Carnegie's 1936 best seller, *How to Win Friends and Influence People,* took liberties with James's writings by proposing that we use only about 10 percent of our brain.

Further contributing to this notion were early studies suggesting that a substantial majority of the cerebral cortex is silent. Advances in the measurement of brain activity now show that these areas are far from silent. They make up what neuroscientists term the brain's "association cortex," which plays a vital function in connecting perceptions, thoughts, and emotions across diverse brain areas.

2 a.m.

Going Against the Clock in Your Brain

The whole world is sleeping—but not shift workers, frequent flyers, or Alzheimer's disease patients. Those whose schedules go against the light-dark cycle of days and nights are up and about, and sometimes not doing so well.

Nearly one in five American workers—about 24 million people— are shift workers, switching work-sleep hours, sometimes several times in one month. Most never truly adjust to having their clocks out of sync, even after twenty years on the job, according to Circadian Technologies, an organization specializing in information and education for the 24/7 workplace. More precisely, their body clocks do not adapt: their brain is telling them they should be asleep when their mind wants them awake.

Almost all shift workers suffer the consequences of night work and shift work. Inner clocks can adjust, but it takes days, and then they may have to adjust again. It's especially hard on those who work rotating shifts, and no wonder: one week, they work 8:00 A.M. to 4:00 P.M.; then their schedule may be changed again from, say, midnight to 8:00 A.M.

Low lights at night may add to the problem. Often occupational safety laws require only 500 lux or so. Researchers have found the transition much easier when the workplace is bathed in at least 1,200 lux of light—the equivalent of what would be found in a bright office.

And the bright lights of dawn create another problem. Each morning when the night shift should be slipping into sleep, daylight is telling their brain its time to get up and go.

Disasters on the Night Shift

Going against the clock—and the perpetual sleepiness that causes—makes night a dangerous time. People are most likely to make mistakes and cause production errors in the predawn "window of circadian low," reports Circadian Technologies.

Executive thinking—your ability to form plans and make decisions and choices—is particularly impaired by sleep loss, research shows. It seems we become less able to deal with new events and changes and less able to evaluate risk accurately.

We also lose some emotional control. When researchers at Harvard University and the University of California, Berkeley, kept adult volunteers awake for about thirty-five hours, magnetic resonance imaging scans showed that sleep deprivation impaired the "rational" prefrontal cortex's control over the amygdala, the brain's emotion center.

This is bad news for medics, military commanders, and parents of small children, and it perhaps explains why casinos stay open all night. Studies and the news confirm that illness, errors, accidents, and just plain bad judgment are much more prevalent on the night shift. That includes everything from minor on-the-job injuries to an increased risk of cancer, death, and a major disaster.

Errors of inattention can be costly, even deadly. Production drops by an estimated 5 percent and the risk of sustaining a serious injury is 43 percent higher on the night shift than on the day shift. Fatalities from human error are especially high during the overnight hours, with work-related deaths more than twice as likely to occur at night.

The times of major disasters tell the tale. The Three Mile Island nuclear power plant crisis in 1979 started between 4:00 A.M. and 6:00 A.M.; the 1968 meltdown at the Chernobyl nuclear power plant began at 1:23 A.M.; the Bhopal chemical plant explosion in India in 1984 was at 12:40 A.M. The *Titanic* hit the ice floe at 11:40 A.M. in 1912; the *Exxon Valdez* oil spill occurred at 12:04 A.M. in 1989; the 2008 train wreck that killed seventy and injured more than four hundred in East China jumped the tracks at 4:38 A.M.

Lack of Sleep Affects Doctors as Much as Alcohol

Sleep deprivation affects the brain just as much in medical care as in factories. Working long hours and shift work is the norm for a medical residency, but studies are showing that lack of sleep has about the same effect on doctors as drinking alcohol. In fact, fatigued residents function as if they'd had three or four cocktails—not what a patient in crisis would prefer.

In one study, J. Todd Arnedt of the University of Michigan and his colleagues measured the performance of thirty-four doctors who had been on call. The volunteers took part in the tests under four different situations, including after working mostly day shifts with only a few overnight calls or after working intense overnight shifts that added up to about eighty hours in a week. For some of the tests, the doctors were given alcoholic drinks or nonalcoholic placebos.

After a month of difficult work schedules, the doctors showed reaction times that were 7 percent slower than their responses after working a lighter schedule. In a driving simulator, doctors coming off a month of working nights showed skills similar to those who had an easier schedule but who had a blood alcohol level just below the legal driving limit. What's more, these doctors were 30 percent more likely to be unable to maintain a steady speed in the driving simulator compared to well-rested doctors who had been drinking.

There was another troubling finding: many sleep-starved residents don't recognize that they're impaired. The concern isn't new. An eighty-hour limit for a resident doctor's workweek was introduced in July 2003 in response to concerns about overwork and its effect on patient care.

Less Sleep? More Fat

To add insult to injury, there's increasing evidence that sleep deprivation can make you fat and keep you from losing weight. It turns out that getting more sleep could mean maintaining a healthier weight and body mass index.

Research has shown that sleep could be a key regulator of body weight because circadian rhythms regulate your metabolism. Animal studies associate radical weight gain with defects in circadian rhythm chemistry.

Sleep also affects levels of two important appetite-regulating hormones: leptin and ghrelin. Leptin is produced by fat cells: low levels signal starvation and a need for a bigger appetite. Ghrelin is an appetite stimulant: the more you have, the more you want to eat.

In a study that began in 1989, researchers collected data on 1,024 volunteers as part of the Wisconsin Sleep Cohort Study. The participants kept records that logged sleep habits, and every four years they had blood tests and underwent tests that measured physiological variables while they slept. Scientists found that people who consistently slept less than five hours a night had significant differences in appetite hormones as compared with people who slept an average of eight hours a night. Sleep-deprived subjects had 16 percent less leptin and nearly 15 percent more ghrelin than those who were well rested.

And pity the poor new mom, wrestling with a pregnancy weight gain and around-the-clock baby demands. It's likely she'll be sleep deprived for months after delivery. But a study shows that women are more likely to lose this "baby fat" in the first six months after giving birth if they get more than five hours of shut-eye a night.

Researchers also found that new moms who slept five or fewer hours a night when their infants were six months old were more likely to retain eleven or more pounds a year after giving birth than those mothers who slumbered for seven hours. In fact, the study showed that getting enough sleep—even just two hours more—may be as important as a healthy diet and exercise for new mothers to return to their prepregnancy weight, says Erica Gunderson, an investigator at Kaiser Permanente Division of Research in Oakland, California, and lead author of the study.

Even children are affected. Johns Hopkins University researchers recently completed a meta-analysis of eleven studies that looked at children's sleep time and their body mass. They found that not getting enough sleep disrupts hormone levels, which may lead to excessive weight gain, the scientists reported in *Obesity.*

Night work alone may mess up weight. People who work night shifts typically eat their main meals at 3:00 or 4:00 A.M., when their cortisol concentrations may not yet be at optimal levels. One theory is that their bodies simply may not be prepared to receive and process food then, so they may not metabolize it efficiently.

Biorhythm and Blues: Faulty Clocks

Night work isn't the only thing depriving some of us of sleep. Stress, sickness, and trauma (physical and mental) also upset our inner clocks, and some of us are born with clocks out of whack or with the genes for time-related illnesses. (See "4:00 A.M.") Chronobiologists (those who study the effects of biological timing) find sleep disturbances connected with many conditions, from cancer to Alzheimer's disease.

In fact, Alzheimer's disease seems to slow things down: the body clock runs late. That means these patients are prone to be up and about in the wee hours, at just the time when caregivers and family are asleep (or want to be). This night roaming is a major reason that some Alzheimer's disease patients are living in care facilities. (See "3:00 A.M.") Yet they may deteriorate even faster in these facilities, and poor lighting may contribute. In the Netherlands, Eus van Someren and his colleagues found that many care facilities for the elderly are dimly lit: afternoon light might measure 27 lux as compared to 50 lux in a normal family living room and 5,000 lux from a winter day.

There is also a rare genetic condition that puts its sufferers permanently in another time zone. Familial advanced sleep phase syndrome is a condition in which sufferers run about four hours before everyone else, waking very early and falling asleep in the early evening (see "4:00 A.M.").

Resetting Your Body Clock

Woe to us when our body clock needs to be reset. When our internal clock gets out of whack or out of sync with the world outside us, we're in trouble. Sleeping and eating become random, thinking can be fuzzy, and emotions unpredictable.

Resetting the body clock isn't as simple as changing the time on your bedside alarm clock: your brain just isn't that nimble. Anyone who has traveled across three or more time zones knows how true this is.

Chronobiologists say it takes days or even weeks to adjust to changes in time zones or in a different time or length of a work shift. Sure, the suprachiasmatic nucleus (that master clock in your brain) can adjust to a new light-dark schedule that will reset your major body clock. But remember those tiny body clocks in other organs? Your brain and body are out of sync in a hundred different places.

When this is a sometime thing, as in jet lag, these many clocks eventually get into sync again. Not all researchers agree that light therapy can speed the reset process, but many doctors suggest that travelers get as much daylight or bright light as possible during the first few days in a new time zone.

But shift workers and other night owls whose ongoing schedules go against the grain have an ongoing problem, even if they get plenty of sleep during the day. Functions ruled by the suprachiasmatic nucleus, such as blood pressure and body temperature, will continue to slumber at night even if their minds are awake and their other body clocks set to a different time zone. It's as if their bodies and brains are living in many different time zones all at once, and it takes a toll: shift workers have a higher incidence of many diseases including, of course, sleep disorders.

3 a.m.

Awake and Anxious

"In the real dark night of the soul, it is always 3 o'clock in the morning, day after day," wrote F. Scott Fitzgerald in *The Crack-Up,* his 1936 book about despair. He certainly knew what he was writing about: everything looks worse in the long, dark hours of the night.

Awake and not wanting to be, you stare at the ceiling, toss and turn, try counting sheep, try counting your breaths, try a warm cup of milk, all to no avail. Worries and regrets overwhelm. Anxiety has its teeth in you, and as you try to get back to sleep and fail, it gnaws away.

You aren't alone there in the dark. More than 40 million others suffer from anxiety disorders, and a goodly number of them are also lying awake at this wee hour while the hobgoblins of stress, anxiety, or dread trample body and mind. More than 18 percent of Americans suffer from some kind of anxiety disorder.

Where the Nightmare Begins
Your anxiety might have begun when you awakened from a nightmare. Not surprisingly, the amygdala—that primitive, alert, and survival-oriented part of your brain—is especially active during dream sleep, a probable cause for anxiety dreams and nightmares. And it probably contributes to the intense anxiety that many people wake up with in the night.

Anxiety is, of course, related to fear and travels the same neurological highways fueled by the same neurochemicals. (See "9:00 P.M.") The difference is that fear has an immediate cause, and usually a resolution. In fact, flat-out fear may be easier to handle than anxiety. We see or hear something dangerous—a wildly veering car, a vicious animal—and our flight-or-flight system goes into overdrive. You react, it comes to an end, and your system settles down to normal.

But anxiety doesn't end so easily. Because it has no focus, it has no resolution. It chews away at us, a diffuse ongoing uneasiness, a tendency to see the worst possible of outcomes, an exaggerated worry and tension that are more intense than the situation warrants. Anxiety can feel like desperate hyperactivity. It may become overgeneralized in a condition called generalized anxiety disorder, leading to living in a state of constant vigilance and dread.

Because anxiety disorders contribute to insomnia, they create a vicious circle. Lack of sleep stimulates anxiety, which keeps you from sleeping, which stimulates more anxiety.

But it can get worse—much worse. You could be having a panic attack. This is anxiety squared—or is it cubed? No matter. It's horrendous.

A False Alarm

One minute you're feeling fine. Then suddenly your heart is racing and pounding, your body is trembling and numb, you feel faint, and your chest hurts. You can't get your breath; you feel as if you're dying. And you may, like thousands of others every year, call 911 or head for the emergency room, sure you are having a heart attack. In fact, you're undergoing a panic attack: a terrifying experience that hits 2 percent of the U.S. population and can strike anyone at any time.

The cause of panic attacks is a mystery. In fact, the average victim of a panic attack sees ten doctors before even getting a diagnosis. One-third who visit a cardiologist with atypical chest pain actually suffer from unrecognized panic disorder.

There are various theories. Family and twin studies show a genetic component that makes some more vulnerable, but genes don't explain all of it. Reminders of traumatic events can trigger attacks in people with posttraumatic stress disorder or some phobias. Overcaffeination might tip your system over the edge. To add to the puzzle, panic attacks in healthy people occur out of the blue.

It might be that your brain believes you're suffocating. Columbia University psychiatrist Donald Klein's "false suffocation alarm" theory suggests some people have an overly sensitive suffocation monitor that sets off false biological alarms in the form of panic attacks when carbon dioxide and sodium lactate levels increase in the brain. More than a decade ago, Klein found that air enriched with carbon dioxide could set off attacks in patients with panic disorders.

In recent research, Eric Griez and his colleagues at the University of Maastricht in the Netherlands had healthy volunteers inhale air with varying levels of carbon dioxide. They found that even these healthy people showed signs of panic in the midst of high levels of carbon

---

DOPAMINE, THE CHEMICAL OF DELIGHT, MAY FUEL DREAD

Who knew? Dopamine, the neurotransmitter linked to pleasure and addiction, may also trigger fear and paranoia.

Scientists have long suspected that dopamine was linked to dread as well as delight. To confirm their suspicions, University of Michigan at Ann Arbor researchers studied what happens to rats when the neurotransmitter is blocked from reaching the rear portion of the nucleus accumbens, where reward-seeking activities and emotions, including fear, are processed.

It seems the animals stayed calm even when scientists also removed glutamate, a neurotransmitter involved in fear. This would ordinarily have sent them into a tizzy, so the finding suggests that too much dopamine in the rear of the nucleus accumbens may be at least partly responsible for dread and also the paranoia that many schizophrenia patients experience, says study coauthor Kent Berridge.

dioxide. The higher the dose of carbon dioxide, the more the participants reported feeling fear and discomfort, as well as a fear of losing control and dying.

Interestingly, these studies go against a commonly held theory that hyperventilation triggers panic attacks. Many people (including some doctors) recommend breathing into paper bags on the theory that rebreathing exhaled, carbon-dioxide-rich air will raise carbon dioxide levels in the blood and stop the panic attack. Turns out that's exactly the wrong thing to do.

That Pill to Fix Your Ills Has a Price

The 1966 Rolling Stones song "Mother's Little Helper" about the power of a little yellow pill is perhaps even more true today than then: more of us, and not just your mama, are finding solace in mood meds. We love our pills.

Back then, it was Valium and other members of the benzodiazepine class of tranquilizing drugs. Today, there's even more to choose from, including the selective serotonin reuptake inhibitor (SSRI) antidepressants, with more mood medications being developed all the time. Newer related medications that aid sleep (two of them are Ambien and Lunesta) are commonly prescribed for people with insomnia, which is often associated with anxiety disorders.

The classic benzodiazepine tranquilizers work by altering the chemical messages that arouse anxiety. They increase the efficiency of gamma-aminobutyric acid (GABA), the most common inhibitory neurotransmitter in the brain. Animal experiments show that targeted delivery of benzodiazepines to the amygdala, which is especially rich in GABA receptors, lessens anxiety. The neurotransmitter serotonin also influences anxiousness. SSRI drugs such as fluoxetine (Prozac) increase levels of serotonin to ease depression and smooth out that moodiness.

But there's a catch. SSRIs need to be taken every day to work. All mood medications work only as long as you take them, and all have some side effects. Some of them, like that cheery little yellow pill, are addictive. When taken with alcohol, they can be fatal.

Calming anxieties is a challenge. There are far many more connections from the amygdala to the thinking brain than the other way around, perhaps giving rational thought little sway. This imbalance is why fears and other emotions can so easily overwhelm us.

The good news is that if you need occasional help getting through the night, benzodiazepines taken short term on an as-needed basis under a doctor's care can help get you over the hump with minimal side effects.

But a better bet might be to eschew the pills and invest in cognitive-behavioral therapy, which has been found to be as effective for anxiety as benzodiazepines and has none of the side effects. This therapy involves gradual exposure to feared situations and learning ways to reduce the catastrophic thinking that is so common in anxiety. This therapy typically yields positive effects in approximately sixteen sessions. Researchers are finding that meditation and exercise can also help. And they're good for the brain too.

3:30 A.M. Night Nurse on Duty

You've been sound asleep for hours, but part of your brain is on sentry duty. Now you hear it: that slight shuffle and clink that inspires more anxiety than fear. It isn't an intruder: it's your aging mom, up again in the night and aimed for who knows where.

For many of us, this sleeping-with-one-eye-open state harkens back to when our kids were waking us in the night. We lost sleep over that, yes. But it was easier to handle a twenty-five-pound toddler who soon outgrew sleep issues than it is to deal with a confused adult who may outweigh you and whose sleeplessness is steadily getting worse. Some of us may be caring for a partner or spouse; others of us are in the so-called sandwich generation, caring for kids and aging parents. None of us with a sleepless loved one are having an easy time of it, including the elder who is up and about in the night.

No doubt, aging eats up sleep time. "If you ask older people about their sleep habits, it becomes clear that many have a harder time sleeping through [the night] than they did when they were younger," says Eus van Someren, a researcher at the Netherlands Institute for Neuroscience in Amsterdam.

Van Someren and his colleagues studied the nerve cells in the suprachiasmatic nucleus that produce vasopressin, a hormone that regulates functions connected with circadian rhythms: body temperature, wakefulness, and activity levels. The team discovered that as we grow older, the number of cells that produce vasopressin decreases. Production of melatonin, the hormone of sleep, decreases as well. As a result, older people generally find it increasingly difficult to keep their internal clock in tune with the day-night cycle, and for those with Alzheimer's disease, it's even worse, since their body clocks tend to run slow, leading to night roaming.

Van Someren and his research team knew that aging rats exposed to bright lights had an increase in vasopressin production and more regular sleeping patterns. Care facilities for the elderly are often gloomy, with a fraction of the light we see in even a winter afternoon. The scientists installed bright full-spectrum lights, prescribed melatonin, and observed 189 Alzheimer's disease patients for up to three and a half years. As suspected, melatonin and light therapy reset some patients' circadian rhythms, and the longer they got the treatment, the better they slept and the more their moods improved.

But another finding surprised the scientists: the mere installation of full-spectrum lamps slowed mental deterioration at least as well as reports of cholinesterase inhibitors—the most prevalent type of drug used to treat Alzheimer's disease. Light combined with melatonin worked even better.

This combination of light therapy and melatonin hasn't consistently helped those with Alzheimer's disease in other studies, but it's promising. With some more tinkering, it might help more of us get to sleep through the night.

4 a.m.

Last Sleep

In these quiet predawn hours, hardly anyone who doesn't want to be awake is up. Most of us are still asleep, snuggled in bed in the dark and running on idle. Breathing and heartbeat are at their slowest, body temperature and blood pressure at their lowest, and our minds are not yet in the waking world.

At this hour, early risers may be heading into REM sleep and ripe for the last dreaming. All night long, we've been cycling through the sleep stages, with the REM stage getting longer every time. Now, near dawn, is the final and longest REM session, the time of the most intense and active dreaming. It will last perhaps twenty to forty minutes, and the dreams you have now are the ones most likely to be remembered when you awake.

It could be that REM sleep prepares us for waking, as we are most vulnerable to being aroused during this sleep stage, awakened by some external stimulus, such as the urge to urinate, a sound, light, or unprovoked erections in men and in women. But most of our conscious selves will lie slumbering for another hour or more, waiting for the rosy fingers of dawn. Brain, mind, and body—awake or asleep—are responding to the powerful body clocks.

4:30 A.M. Awake So Early? You May Be an Unlucky Lark

Some brains have to get up early for work. Some may be awake because they have a new baby, a job on the night shift, or a red-eye flight, or they have been partying the night away.

Unfortunately, some brains run against the circadian clock and everybody else's sense of time. It can be a temporary condition brought on by jet lag, insomnia, or sickness or trauma (physical or mental). Age has an effect. Seniors, for example, who sleep fewer hours, tend to be up when the rest of the world is down: 4:00 A.M. is a common waking time, perhaps instigated by weaker bladders and aging prostates and the urge to urinate. Alzheimer's disease and dementia patients are notorious night roamers.

And some are born with clocks so out of whack that they are practically living in another time zone. These people suffer from a rare and unfortunate condition written in their genes: familial advanced sleep phase syndrome (FASPS), in which they hit the hay and wake up on a cycle about four hours before everyone else. Falling asleep at 7:00 P.M., they are arising at 4:00 A.M., giving "early to bed and early to rise" a whole new meaning.

FASPS affects only 0.3 percent of the population. Scientists discovered the inherited problem by studying a large family in Utah. Looking at how the circadian clock goes awry for FASPS, researchers found that a mutation in a clock gene that helps regulate the circadian rhythm is to blame and that a simple expulsion of protein from the cell nucleus seems to be at the root of the syndrome. The change in the protein encoded by the mutant PER2 gene is quite subtle: a single protein building block, or amino acid, is changed from a serine to a glycine.

The end result is not so subtle: a speeded-up sleep-wake cycle and a brain that would be good at jobs requiring very early waking, such as farmwork. Or parenting.

Your Brain Tomorrow

It's a new dawn, and your brain will wake you up soon. As you go about this new day, it will guide you through many processes familiar from the days before, especially the most basic.

But you won't be exactly the same person tomorrow as you were today. Neuroscientists are just beginning to discover all of the ways a living brain can be transformed by new experiences, emotions, and actions and the ways an ailing brain can be helped by surgery, pharmacology, and technology.

We've learned more about the brain in the past fifty years than in the previous five thousand. What was considered science fiction a decade ago is fact today, and more findings are on the horizon.

The detailed workings of your brain remain the last great mystery of the body. But neurology research has been accelerating at ever faster rates as we learn more about genetics and as new techniques are developed for imaging, understanding, and treating the brain.

History is conspiring with science right now to support a unique era for brain research. Propelled by the growing demands of the aging boomer population bulge, there's a tremendous push for more answers to Alzheimer's disease, dementia, and other issues of the aging brain. The mass of soldiers returning from wars in Iraq and Afghanistan with catastrophic head injuries and missing limbs has spurred groundbreaking work in areas of brain trauma and neurally operated lifelike prosthetics.

These practical applications certainly inspire us to learn more about the workings of the brain and how we can understand and harness its immense powers to help with the processes and problems of daily life.

But scientists are also searching for answers to more knotty and universal questions, such as how a flesh-and-blood physical system is connected to the intangible mind, spirit, and soul that gives meaning to life, how we make art and feel love (and why we care about either), and how your brain is molded by your thoughts, including, possibly, by reading this book.

Sources

The sources are listed by subhead in the order they appear in each chapter.

Introduction

You Gotta Know the Territory: Adapted from "Brain Basics: Know Your Brain" from the National Institute of Neurological Disorders and Stroke, http://www.ninds.nih.gov/disorders/brain_basics/know_your_brain.htm#fore.

Why Does Your Brain Use So Much Power? Adapted from Nikhil Swaminathan, "Why Does the Brain Need So Much Power? New Study Shows Why the Brain Drains So Much of the Body's Energy," *Scientific American,* Apr. 29, 2008, http://www.sciam.com/article.cfm?id=why-does-the-brain-need-s.

Your Neurotransmitters: Adapted in part from "Brain Basics: Know Your Brain" and other National Institutes of Health articles and glossaries.

Do You Need Only Half a Brain? Adapted from Charles Q. Choi, "Do You Need Only Half Your Brain?" *Scientific American,* Mar. 2008.

Charting the Day. Excerpted and adapted from several sources, including Karen Wright, "Times of Our Lives: The Science of Staying Young," by *Scientific American Special Edition,* June 2004, and Ulrich Kraft, "Rhythm and Blues," *Scientific American Mind,* June–July 2007.

The Best of Times?: Excerpted from several sources, including Michael W. Young, "The Tick-Tock of the Biological Clock," *Scientific American,* Mar.

2000; and Karen Wright, "The Times of Our Lives: The Science of Staying Young," *Scientific American Special Edition*, June 2004.

5:00 A.M.
Your Inner Alarm Clocks: Adapted from Gerhard Roth, "The Quest to Find Consciousness," *Scientific American Mind*, Jan. 2004.

Your Brain Chemicals: Adapted from Roth, "The Quest to Find Consciousness."

Larks and Owls: Adapted from J. A. Horne and O. A. Ostberg, "Self-Assessment Questionnaire to Determine Morningness-Eveningness in Human Circadian Rhythms," *International Journal of Chronobiology*, 1976, 4(2), 97–110.

Why Do Men Awake with Erections? Adapted in part from Irwin Goldstein, "Male Sexual Circuitry," *Scientific American*, Aug. 2000.

An Orchestra of Sensory Harmony: Smell and taste information adapted from R. Douglas Fields, "Sex and the Secret Nerve," *Scientific American Mind*, Feb.–Mar. 2007.

The Very Smell of Coffee May Help the Rat Race: Adapted from Steve Mirsky, "Just Smelling Coffee Helps Head," *Scientific American*, June 25, 2008, http://www.sciam.com/podcast/episode.cfm?id=BD2F8686-0B3F-0458-FA282 5CF5B2E71DF. Han-Seok Seo and others, "Effects of Coffee Bean Aroma on the Rat Brain Stressed by Sleep Deprivation: A Selected Transcript- and 2D Gel-Based Proteome Analysis," *Journal of Agriculture and Food Chemistry*, 2008, *56*, 4665–4673.

Touch and Movement: Adapted from Steven Brown and Lawrence M. Parsons, "The Neuroscience of Dance," *Scientific American*, July 2008. Martin Grunwald, "Worlds of Feeling," *Scientific American Mind*, Dec. 2004.

Varieties of Touch: Adapted from Grunwald, "Worlds of Feeling." Jamie Talan, "Bonding Hormone," *Scientific American Mind*, Feb.–Mar. 2006.

Your Brain Prefers Autopilot: Adapted from Roth, "The Quest to Find Consciousness."

Background information: Roth, "The Quest to Find Consciousness." National Sleep Foundation, http://www.sleepfoundation.org/site/c.huIXKjM0IxF/b .2417141/k.C60C/Welcome.htm. Karen Wright, "Times of Our Lives," *Scientific American Special Edition*, June 2004.

6:00 A.M.

The Seat of Consciousness: Adapted from Gerhard Roth, "The Quest to Find Consciousness," *Scientific American Mind,* Jan. 2004.

Big-Brained Bamboozlers: Adapted from David Livingstone Smith, "Natural Born Liars: Big-Brained Bamboozlers," *Scientific American Mind,* June 2005.

Emotion, Memory, and Consciousness: Adapted from Roth, "The Quest to Find Consciousness."

It's Always About Networking: Adapted from Roth, "The Quest to Find Consciousness."

Little Gray Cells and Big White Matter: Adapted from R. Douglas Fields, "White Matter Matters," *Scientific American,* Mar. 2008. George Bartzokis and others, "Lifespan Trajectory of Myelin Integrity and Maximum Motor Speed," *Neurobiology of Aging,* Oct. 16, 2008.

Why Does the Outer Surface of the Brain Have Folds? Adapted from Claus C. Hilgetag and Helen Barbas, "Why Does the Outer Surface of the Brain Have Folds?" *Scientific American,* June–July 2007.

7:00 A.M.

Reason Needs a Neurochemical Boost: Adapted from Strueber, Lueck, and Roth, "The Violent Brain." Molly J. Crockett and others, "Serotonin Modulates Behavioral Reactions to Unfairness," *Science,* June 27, 2008, p. 1739.

Can Meditation Help Master Those Emotions? Adapted from Isis Mauss, "Control Your Anger," *Scientific American Mind,* Dec. 2005. Jamie Talan, "Science Probes Spirituality," *Scientific American Mind,* Feb.–Mar. 2006.

Is There a God Spot in Your Brain? Adapted from David Biello, "Searching for God in the Brain," *Scientific American Mind,* Oct.–Nov. 2007.

Practice Makes Compassion: Adapted from David Biello, "Meditate on This: You Can Learn to Be More Compassionate," *Scientific American Online,* Mar. 26, 2008, http://www.sciam.com/article.cfm?id=meditate-on-this-you -can-learn-to-be-more-compassionate.

Background information: David Strueber, Monika Lueck, and Gerhard Roth, "The Violent Brain," *Scientific American Mind,* Dec. 2006–Jan. 2007.

8:00 A.M.

Finding Your Way: Adapted from James J. Knierim, "The Matrix in Your Head," *Scientific American Mind,* June–July 2007.

Why His Brain May Not Ask Directions: Adapted from Larry Cahill, "His Brain, Her Brain," *Scientific American,* May 2005.

Been There, Done That: Adapted from "Could Déjà Vu Be Explained by Grid Cells Ask the Experts," *Scientific American Online,* Apr. 2008, http://www.sciam.com/article.cfm?id=could-deja-vu-be-explained-by-grid-cells.

How We Know Where to Find Our Lost Keys: Adapted from Nikhil Swaminathan, "How We Know Where Our Lost Keys Are," *Scientific American Online,* July 20, 2007, http://www.sciam.com/article.cfm?id=feature-based-attention.

9:00 A.M.

That Face, That Familiar Face: Adapted from Nina Bublitz, "A Face in the Crowd," *Scientific American Mind,* Apr.–May 2008.

Friend or Foe? Adapted from Marion Sonnenmoser, "Friend or Foe?" *Scientific American Mind,* Apr. 2005. Siri Schubert, "A Look Tells All," *Scientific American Mind,* Oct.–Nov. 2006. Nicole Branan, "She Never Forgets a Face, *Scientific American Mind,* June–July 2008.

Are You My Mother? Adapted from Thomas Grueter, "Forgetting Faces," *Scientific American Mind,* Aug.–Sept. 2007.

Mirror, Mirror: Adapted from David Dobbs, "A Revealing Reflection," *Scientific American Mind,* Apr.–May 2006.

The Broken Mirror: Adapted in part from David Dobbs, "A Revealing Reflection," *Scientific American Mind,* Apr.–May 2006. A. J. Imke and others, "Neurons in the Fusiform Gyrus Are Fewer and Smaller in Autism," *Brain,* 2008, *131*(4), 987–999.

Tip of the Tongue Moments: Adapted from Nicole Branan, "Wait Don't Tell Me," *Scientific American Mind,* Apr.–May 2008.

If I Could Read Your Mind: Social Cognition Research by Roberta Saxe. MIT news release by Anne Trafton, "Thought Provoker: MIT's Rebecca Saxe Probes Mechanics of Judgment, Beliefs," *MIT News Office,* May 14, 2008.

10:00 A.M.

Stress in the Brain: Adapted from Hermann Englert, "Sussing Out Stress," *Scientific American Mind*, Jan. 2004.

Stress Destroys Neurons: Adapted from Nicole Branan, ". . . And Stress Kills Them Off," *Scientific American Mind*, June–July 2007.

Stress Ups the Risk of Alzheimer's Disease: Adapted from Nicole Branan, "Anxiety and Alzheimer's," *Scientific American Mind*, Oct.–Nov. 2007.

The Very Thought of It Is Enough: Adapted from Robert Sapolsky, "Taming Stress," *Scientific American*, Sept. 2003.

Multitasking—Again? and The Limits of Multitasking: Adapted from Klaus Manhart, "The Limits of Multitasking," *Scientific American Mind*, Dec. 2004.

How Your Brain Helps Your Job Kill You: Adapted from Christine Soares, "How Your Job Is Killing You," *Scientific American*, Apr. 2008.

Fighting Fire with Fire: Using Stress Hormones to Lower Stress. Adapted from Jonathan Beard, "Fighting Stress with Stress Hormones," *Scientific American Mind*, Apr.–May 2007.

You Can Lull Your Brain Away from Stress: Adapted from Jonathan Beard, "Fighting Stress with Stress Hormones," *Scientific American Mind*, Apr.–May 2007.

Flow Versus Stress: Adapted in part from J. R. Minkel, "Improvising a Jazz Tune Puts the Brain in an Altered State," *Scientific American Online*, May 2008, http://www.sciam.com/article.cfm?id=improvising-a-jazz-tune.

Background information: Mihaly Csíkszentmihályi, *Finding Flow: The Psychology of Engagement with Everyday Life* (New York: Basic Books, 1998); and *Flow: The Psychology of Optimal Experience* (New York: Harper Perennial, 1991).

11:00 A.M.

The Brain's CEO: Adapted from Brian Levine, "Brian Wilson: A Cork on the Ocean," *Scientific American Mind*, Dec. 2005.

"Chemo Brain" Can Ambush Your CEO: Adapted from Roberta Friedman, "'Chemo Brain' Culprit," *Scientific American Mind*, Feb.–Mar. 2008.

Choosing Economically: Based on Michael Shermer, "Free to Choose," *Scientific American Online,* Mar. 2007, http://www.sciam.com/article.cfm?id =free-to-choose.

Does Price Affect Your Wine Choice? Adapted from Graciela Flores, "Paying for Pleasure," *Scientific American Mind,* Apr.–May 2008.

Making an Emotional Moral Choice: Adapted from Graciela Flores, "Emotional Morality," *Scientific American Mind,* June–July 2007.

Choosing Wearies Your Brain: Adapted from On Amir, "Tough Choices: How Making Decisions Tires Your Brain," *Scientific American Online,* July 22, 2008, http://www.sciam.com/article.cfm?id=tough-choices-how-making. Kathleen D. Vohs and others, "Making Choices Impairs Subsequent Self-Control: A Limited-Resource Account of Decision Making, Self-Regulation, and Active Initiative," *Journal of Personality and Social Psychology,* 2008, *94,* 883–898.

The Brain Has a Section for Regret: Adapted from "Brain Region Tied to Regret Identified," *Scientific American Online,* Aug. 8, 2005, http://www.sciam .com/article.cfm?id=brain-region-tied-to-regr.

Background information: When Morality Is Hard to Like: Jorge Moll and Ricardo De Oliveira-Souza, "How Do We Juggle Evidence and Emotions to Make a Moral Decision?" *Scientific American Mind,* Feb.–Mar. 2008.

Noon

How Hunger Works in Your Brain: Adapted from Oliver Grimm, "Addicted to Food?" *Scientific American Mind,* Apr.–May 2007.

We're Losing Our Scents: Adapted from Coco Ballantyne, "Losing Scents," *Scientific American,* Dec. 2007.

Still Hungry? Adapted from Oliver Grimm, "Addicted to Food?" *Scientific American Mind,* Apr.–May 2007.

Why Calories Taste Delicious: Zane B. Andrews and Tamas L. Horvath, "Eating and the Brain." Mind Matters, *Scientific American Online.* Sept. 30, 2008, http:// www.sciam.com/article.cfm?id=why-calories-are-delicious&print=true.

Addicted to _____ (Fill in the Blank): Adapted in part from Eric J. Nestler and Robert C. Malenka, "The Addicted Brain," *Scientific American,* Mar. 2004.

Self-Control Sucks Your Energy: Adapted from Siri Carpenter, "Fuel for Thought," *Scientific American,* June–July 2007.

Yes, There Is Such a Thing as Brain Food: Adapted from Ingrid Kiefer, "Brain Food," *Scientific American Monday,* Oct.–Nov. 2007.

Your Appetite Regulator Might Be Rewritable: Adapted from J. R. Minkel, "Rewritable Appetite," *Scientific American,* June 2004.

1:00 P.M.

Partial Recall: Adapted from Nikhil Swaminathan, "Partial Recall: Why Memory Fades with Age," *Scientific American Online,* Dec. 5, 2007, http://www.sciam.com/article.cfm?id=partial-recall-why-memory-fades.

Can You Help Your Brain Stay Young(er)? Source: V. C. Crooks and others, "Social Network, Cognitive Function, and Dementia Incidence Among Elderly Women," *American Journal of Public Health,* 2008, *98*(7), 1221–1227.

Predicting Alzheimer's Disease: Adapted from Peter Sergo, "Predicting Alzheimer's," *Scientific American Mind,* Feb.–Mar. 2008.

How Forgetting Is Good for the Brain. Excerpted from Melinda Wenner, "Forgetting to Remember," Head Lines, *Scientific American Mind,* Oct.–Nov. 2007.

Got Degrees? Adapted from Sara Goudarzi, "Double-Edged Sword," *Scientific American Mind,* Feb.–Mar. 2008.

Asleep at the Wheel—Almost? Adapted from Joachim Marschall, "Seduced by Sleep," *Scientific American Mind,* Feb.–Mar. 2007.

1:54 P.M. Just Time for a Six-Minute Power Nap: Adapted from John Whitfield, "Naps for Better Recall," *Scientific American,* May 2008.

2:00 P.M.

Can't Get No Satisfaction? Adapted from Aribert Rothenberger and Tobias Banaschewski, "Informing the ADHD Debate," *Scientific American Mind,* Dec. 2004. Turhan Canli, "The Character Code," *Scientific American Mind,* Feb.–Mar. 2008.

Risky Business: Adapted from Klaus Manhart, "Lust for Danger," *Scientific American Mind,* Oct. 2005.

ADHD and Risk Taking Could Be Good—Sometimes: Adapted in part from Cynthia Graber, "ADHD Genetics Sometimes Beneficial," *Scientific American*, 60-second podcast, June 13, 2008, http://www.sciam.com/podcast/episode.cfm?id=800F0FCD-F580-32F3-65A672BF6C41085D.

Maybe We're Born with a Wandering Brain: Adapted from Mason Inman, "The Prodigal Mind," *Scientific American Mind*, Apr.–May 2007.

Wired and Hooked: Excerpted in part from Robert Kubey and Mihaly Csikszentmihályi, "Television Addiction Is No Mere Metaphor," *Scientific American Mind*, Jan. 2004. Jonah Lehrer, "Brain Flashes: Three Cognitive News Items You Might Have Missed," *Scientific American Online*, June 17, 2008, http://www.sciam.com/article.cfm?id=brain-flashes-three-cogni/.

Background information: Attention Deficit Hyperactivity Disorder (ADHD). National Institute of Mental Health Booklet. http://www.nimh.nih.gov/health/publications/attention-deficit-hyperactivity-disorder/index.shtml. Statistics: Centers for Disease Control and Prevention: Attention-Deficit/Hyperactivity Disorder (ADHD). http://www.cdc.gov/ncbddd/adhd/. Anna Gosline, "Bored?" *Scientific American Mind*, Dec. 2007–Jan. 2008.

3:00 P.M.

Background information: Your Pain Is Mainly in the Brain: Adapted from Allan I. Basbaum and David Julius, "Toward Better Pain Control," *Scientific American*, June 2006.

How Pain Hurts Your Brain: Adapted in part from Lisa Melton, "Aching Atrophy," *Scientific American*, Jan. 2004.

Mind Under Matter, Mind over Brain: Adapted in part from Kat Leitzell, "Mind Under Matter," *Scientific American Mind*, Oct.–Nov. 2007; Hunter G. Hoffman, "Virtual Reality Therapy," *Scientific American*, Aug. 2004; Kiryn Haslinger, "Placebo Power," *Scientific American Mind*, Dec. 2005.

Your Brain Itself Has No Pain: Adapted from Mark A. W. Andrews, "Why Doesn't the Human Brain Have Pain Receptors?" *Scientific American Mind*, Apr.–May 2007.

Is Hypnosis Real? Adapted from Grant Benham and Michael R. Nash, "Is Hypnosis Real?" *Scientific American Mind*, June–July 2007.

The United States Is a Country in Pain: Excerpted from the Editors, "People in Pain," *Scientific American,* July 2008.

A Window into Traumatic Forgetting: Amanda J. Barnier, Rochelle E. Cox, and Greg Savage, "Hypnosis, Memory and the Brain," *Scientific American Online.* Oct. 7, 2008, http://www.sciam.com/article.cfm?id=hypnosis-memory -brain&print=true.

Sticking Point: Adapted from Susanne Kemmer, "Sticking Point," *Scientific American Mind,* Feb.–Mar. 2007.

4:00 P.M.

Exercise Grows Neurons and Improves Memory: Adapted from Melinda Wenner, "Exercising Generates New Brain Cells . . . ," *Scientific American Mind,* June–July 2007.

Why We Get Food Cravings: Adapted from Peter Pressman and Roger Clemens, "Why Do We Get Food Cravings?" *Scientific American Mind,* Oct.– Nov. 2006.

The Most Dangerous Time for Teens: Statistics from Office of Juvenile Justice and Delinquency Prevention. *Juvenile Offenders and Victims: 1997 Update on Violence.* http://ojjdp.ncjrs.org/pubs/juvoff/time.html.

The Teen Brain Is Still Changing: Adapted from The National Institute of Mental Health, "Teenage Brain: A Work in Progress." Jan. 2009. http://www .nimh.nih.gov/health/publications/teenage-brain-a-work-in-progress-fact- sheet/index.shtml.

But Don't Forget Hormones: Adapted from Nikhil Swaminathan, "Whatever! Hormonal Reversal During Puberty Keeps Teens Totally Anxious," *Scientific American Online,* Mar. 12, 2007, http://www.sciam.com/article.cfm?id =hormone-reverses-in-puberty-causing-anxiety.

Background information: S. Whittle and others, "Prefrontal and Amygdala Volumes Are Related to Adolescents' Affective Behaviors During Parent- Adolescent Interactions," *Proceedings of the National Academy of Sciences,* Feb. 25, 2008.

5:00 P.M.

Is It Really Depression? General depression information: Walter Brown, "Good News About Depression," *Scientific American Mind,* June–July 2007. National Institute of Mental Health, "Depression," Mar. 6, 2009, http://www .nimh.nih.gov/health/topics/depression/index.shtml.

Searching for the Pathway to Depression: Adapted from J. R. Minkel, "Brain Pathway May Underlie Depression," *Scientific American Online,* July 6, 2007, http://www.sciam.com/article.cfm?id=brain-pathway-may-underlie-depression.

Maybe You're Just SAD: Excerpts from Ulrich Kraft, "Lighten Up," *Scientific American Mind,* Oct. 2005. Adapted from Lisa Conti, "How Light Deprivation Causes Depression," *Scientific American Mind Online,* Aug. 8, 2008, http://www.sciam.com/article.cfm?id=down-in-the-dark.

Magnetic Energy May Work When Meds Fail: Adapted from Erica Westly, "A Magnetic Boost: Activating Certain Neurons May Alleviate Depression," *Scientific American Mind,* Apr.–May 2008.

A Peak Time for Suicide: Adapted from Carol Ezzell, "Why? The Neuroscience of Suicide," *Scientific American,* Feb. 2003.

Good Grief: Addicted to Grieving: Adapted from Nicole Branan, "Addicted to Grief?" *Scientific American Online,* July 17, 2008, http://www.sciam.com/article.cfm?id=addicted-to-grief&print=true. And in *Scientific American Mind,* Oct.–Nov. 2008.

6:00 P.M.

An Oxytocin High: Adapted from Paul J. Zak, "The Neurobiology of Trust," *Scientific American,* June 2008.

Nobody Home? Adapted from Victoria Stern, "So Lonely It Hurts," *Scientific American Mind,* May–June 2008.

Pat the Bunny: Information from Mizzou Alumni Association, the University of Missouri. Randy Mertens, "Lady Jane, the Robot Dog," Apr. 2003, http://atmizzou.missouri.edu/apr03/RobotDog.htm.

A Close Circle of Friends: Adapted from Klaus Manhart, "Good Friends," *Scientific American Mind,* Apr.–May 2008.

Oh, Those Comforting Cravings: National Institute of Drug Abuse. "Drugs, Brains, and Behavior—The Science of Addiction." Feb. 19, 2009, http://www.drugabuse.gov/scienceofaddiction/.

Bottoms Up. Where Many Alcoholics End: Adapted from John I. Nurnberger and Laura Jean Bieret, "Seeking the Connections: Alcoholism and Our Genes," *Scientific American,* Apr. 2007.

Is Addiction the Result Rather Than the Cause of Brain Damage? Adapted from Thania Benios, "Predisposition for Addiction," *Scientific American Mind,* June–July 2007.

How Alcohol Steals Your Sense of Humor: Adapted from Jonathan Beard, "Drinking Is No Joke," *Scientific American Mind,* Apr.–May 2007.

Still Crazy After All These Years? Adapted from Peter Brown, "When I'm Sixty Four," *Scientific American,* May 2008.

Background information: Eric J. Nestler and Robert C. Malenka, "The Addicted Brain," *Scientific American,* Mar. 2004. Alcoholism Staying Sober 2006. National Institute on Drug Abuse, "Drugs, Brains, and Behavior: The Science of Addiction," Feb. 19, 2009, http://www.drugabuse.gov/scienceofaddiction/.

7:00 P.M.

The Musical Path to the Brain: Adapted from Eckart O. Altenmüller, "Music in Your Head," *Scientific American Mind,* Jan. 2004. Norman M. Weinberger, "Music and the Brain," *Scientific American,* Nov. 2004.

Music Survives Brain Damage: Adapted from Weinberger, "Music and the Brain." American Society of Hypertension's Twenty Third Annual Scientific Meeting and Exposition (ASH 2008). Pietro A. Modesti, MD, PhD, University of Florence, Italy.

How the Brain Hears over Din: Excerpted from Christopher Intagliata, "How the Brain Hears over Din," *Scientific American,* June 11, 2008, 60-second podcast, http://www.sciam.com/podcast/episode.cfm?id=761dae19-D6e1-Df18-2ce26ef992b24d2a.

Your Brain Expands to Store Music: Adapted from Weinberger, "Music and the Brain."

So You Think You Can Dance? Adapted from Steven Brown and Lawrence M. Parsons, "The Neuroscience of Dance," *Scientific American*, July 2008.

Born to Rock? Adapted from Weinberger, "Music and the Brain."

The Creative Brain and Right Brain, Left Brain? Adapted from Ulrich Kraft, "Unleashing Creativity," *Scientific American Mind*, Apr. 2005.

Tango to Better Balance: Adapted from Brown and Parsons, "The Neuroscience of Dance."

Don't Oversimplify That Right Brain Stuff: Adapted from Scott O. Lilienfeld and Hal Arkowitz, "Uncovering 'Brainscams': In Which the Authors Debunk Myths Concerning the Three-Pound Organ Inside Our Head," *Scientific American Mind*, Feb.–Mar. 2008.

The Musical Ear Is Learned, Not Born: Adapted from E. H. Margulis and others, "Selective Neurophysiologic Responses to Music in Instrumentalists with Different Listening Biographies," *Human Brain Mapping*, Dec. 10, 2007, pp. 267–275.

8:00 P.M.

The Best Medicine: Adapted from Charmaine Liebertz, "A Healthy Laugh," *Scientific American Mind*, Oct. 2005.

Tracking Your Internal Laugh Track: Adapted from Marina Krakovsky, "Sitcoms on the Brain," *Scientific American*, June 2004. C. M. Cripps et al., Understanding Social Dysfunction in the Behavioural Variant of Fronto-temporal Dementia: The Role of Emotion and Sarcasm Processing," *Brain*, Oct. 2008.

The Aha! Moment: Adapted from Peter Sergo, "The Eyes Get It," *Scientific American Mind*, Apr.–May 2008.

TV Addiction Is No Mere Metaphor: Adapted from Robert Kubey and Mihaly Csikszentmihályi, "Television Addiction Is No Mere Metaphor," *Scientific American Mind*, Jan. 2004.

9:00 P.M.

How Fear Works in Your Brain: Background information: David Dobbs, "Mastery of Emotions," *Scientific American Mind,* Feb.–Mar. 2006. Rüdiger Vaas, "Fear Not," *Scientific American Special Edition,* Jan. 2004.

Who's Afraid? Adapted from Nikhil Swaminathan, "Who's Afraid? Not These Brain Cells," *Scientific American Online,* July 11, 2008, http://www.sciam.com/article.cfm?id=whos-afraid-not-these-brain-cells-2008-07-11&print=true.

When the Brain Decides It's Time to Scram: Adapted from Nikhil Swaminathan, "Fear Factor: When the Brain Decides It's Time to Scram," *Scientific American Online,* Aug. 23, 2007, http://www.sciam.com/article.cfm?id=the-brain-fear-factor.

Time Seems to Stand Still in Fear: Adapted from "The Slow Down of Time in Crisis," *Scientific American Online,* 60-second podcast, Dec. 13, 2007, http://www.sciam.com/podcast/episode.cfm?id=D4146F12-E7F2-99DF-38CD1FEB89C4057C&print=true.

The Many Parts of a Violent Brain: Basics adapted and excerpted from Turhan Canli, "Genes of the Psyche: The Character Code," *Scientific American Mind,* Feb.–Mar. 2008.

The Testosterone Connection: Adapted from Strueber, Lueck, and Roth, "The Violent Brain."

Background information: Daniel Strueber, Monika Lueck, and Gerhard Roth, "The Violent Brain," *Scientific American Mind,* Dec. 2006–Jan. 2007. Violent crime risk from U.S. Department of Justice and other reports.

10:00 P.M.

Your Brain on Sex: Adapted from Portner, "The Orgasmic Mind."

Women, Men, and Orgasms: How Alike Are They? Lisa M. Diamond, "Female Bisexuality from Adolescence to Adulthood: Results from a 10-Year Longitudinal Study," *Developmental Psychology,* 2008, *44*(1), 5–14.

Does the Penis Have a Brain of Its Own? Adapted from Irwin Goldstein, "Male Sexual Circuitry." Adapted from Portner, "The Orgasmic Mind."

A Kiss Is More Than Just a Kiss: Adapted from Chip Walter, "Fast Facts: Kiss and Tell, Affairs of the Lips," *Scientific American Mind*, Feb.–Mar. 2008.

What's Love Got to Do with It? Adapted from Melinda Wenner, "Sex Is Better for Women in Love," *Scientific American Mind*, Feb.–Mar. 2008.

Are You Born Gay? Nikhil Swaminathan, "Study Says Brains of Gay Men and Women Are Similar," *Scientific American Online*, June 16, 2008, http://www .sciam.com/article.cfm?id=study-says-brains-of-gay.

Background information: Martin Portner, "The Orgasmic Mind," *Scientific American Mind*, Apr.–May 2008. Irwin Goldstein, "Male Sexual Circuitry," *Scientific American*, Aug. 2000.

11:00 P.M.

The Five Stages of Sleep: Adapted from Jerome R. Siegel, "Why We Sleep," *Scientific American*, Nov. 2003; National Institute of Neurological Disorders and Stroke, "Brain Basics: Understanding Sleep," May 2007, http://www .ninds.nih.gov/disorders/brain_basics/understanding_sleep.htm.

How Long Can Someone Stay Awake? Adapted from Christian Gillin, "How Long Can Humans Stay Awake?" *Scientific American*, July 2002.

Insomnia: Adapted from Henry Olders, "What Causes Insomnia?" *Scientific American Mind*, Feb.–Mar. 2006.

Perhaps Less Is More? Adapted from Older, "What Causes Insomnia?"

Interrupted Sleep? Adapted from Walter A. Brown, "Ancient Sleep in Modern Times," *Scientific American Mind*, Dec. 2006–Jan. 2007.

Call Me Sleepless: Adapted from R. Douglas Fields, "Call Me Sleepless," *Scientific American Mind*, Aug.–Sept. 2008.

Still Awake? Adapted from Molly Webster, "Can You Catch Up on Lost Sleep?" *Scientific American*, May 6, 2008, http://www.sciam.com/article.cfm ?id =fact-or-fiction-can-you-catch-up-on-sleep.

Is Insomnia Worse for Night Owls? Adapted from J. R. Minkel, "Insomnia Worse for Night Owls," *Scientific American*, Apr. 15, 2007, www.sciam.com /article.cfm?id=insomnia-worse-for-night.

Background information: National Sleep Foundation: http://www.sleepfounda tion.org. National Institute of Neurological Disorders and Stroke: "Brain Basics: Understanding Sleep," May 2007, http://www.ninds.nih.gov/disorders/brain _basics/understanding_sleep.htm.

Midnight

Strolling in Your Sleep: Adapted from Antonio Oliviero, "Why Do Some People Sleepwalk?" *Scientific American Mind,* Feb.–Mar. 2008.

Drifting into Dreamland: Adapted from Gerhard Klösch and John P. Dittam, "Why Do We Dream?" *Scientific American Mind,* Dec. 2007–Jan. 2008.

Will You Die Without REM Sleep? Adapted from Christie Nicholson, "Strange But True: Less Sleep Means More Dreams," *Scientific American Online,* Sept. 20, 2007, http://www.sciam.com/article.cfm?id=strange-but-true-less -sleep-means-more-dreams.

Do Banished Thoughts Resurface in Dreams? Adapted from Alla Katsnelson, "Banished Thoughts Resurface in Dreams," *Scientific American Online,* Mar. 24, 2004, http://www.sciam.com/article.cfm?id=banished-thoughts-resurfa.

Want to Dream More? Adapted from Nicholson, "Strange But True."

Background information: Jonathan Winson, "The Meaning of Dreams," *Scientific American Special Edition,* Aug. 2002. Jerome M. Siegel, "Why We Sleep," *Scientific American,* Nov. 2003. Gerhard Klösch and Ulrich Kraft, "Sweet Dreams Are Made of This," *Scientific American Mind,* June 2005.

1:00 A.M.

Cleaning Up Your Neural Garbage: Adapted from Daniel J. Klionsky and Vojo Deretic, "How Cells Clean House," *Scientific American,* May 2008.

Why Your Brain Doesn't Take a Break Already: Robert Stickgold and Jeffrey M. Ellenbogen, "Quiet! Sleeping Brain at Work," *Scientific American Mind,* Aug.–Sept. 2008.

Stimulating the Sleeping Brain Might Boost Memory: Adapted from Jonathan Beard, "Hardwiring Memories," *Scientific American Mind,* Feb.–Mar. 2007.

The 10 Percent Myth: Adapted from Scott O. Lilienfeld and Hal Arkowitz, "Uncovering 'Brainscams': In Which the Authors Debunk Myths Concerning the Three-Pound Organ Inside Our Head," *Scientific American Mind*, Feb.–Mar. 2008.

Background information: National Institute of Neurological Disorders and Stroke, "What Does Sleep Do for Us?" May 2007, http://www.ninds.nih .gov/disorders/brain_basics/understanding_sleep.htm. Robert Stickgold and Jeffrey M. Ellenbogen, "Quiet! Sleeping Brain at Work," *Scientific American Mind*, Aug.–Sept. 2008. John Whitfield, "Naps for Better Recall," *Scientific American*, May 2008. V. V. Vyazovskiy, "Molecular and Electrophysiological Evidence for Net Synaptic Potentiation in Wake and Depression in Sleep," *Nature Neuroscience*, 2008, *11*(2), 200–208.

2:00 A.M.

Disasters on the Night Shift: Information from Circadian Technologies and from Katherine Leitzell, "Irritable? Take a Nap," *Scientific American Mind*, Feb.–Mar. 2008.

Lack of Sleep Affects Doctors as Much as Alcohol: Adapted from Sarah Graham, "Lack of Sleep Affects Doctors Like Alcohol Does," *Scientific American*, Sept. 7, 2005, http://www.sciam.com/article.cfm?id=lack-of-sleep-affects-doc.

Less Sleep? More Fat: Adapted from Sarah Graham, "Sleep Deprivation Tied to Shifts in Hunger Hormones," *Scientific American Online*, Dec. 7, 2004, http://www.sciam.com/article.cfm?id=sleep-deprivation-tied-to. "Want to Lose Baby Fat? Sleep on It," *Scientific American Online*, Nov. 23, 2007, http://www.sciam .com/article.cfm?id=news-bytes-us-china-environment. The Editors, "More Sleep, Less Fat," *Scientific American*, Apr. 2008.

Biorhythm and Blues: Adapted from Kraft, "Rhythm and Blues," *Scientific American Mind*, June–July 2007.

Resetting Your Body Clock: Adapted from Karen Wright, "Times of Our Lives," *Scientific American Special Edition*, June 2004.

Background information: Workplace statistics from Circadian Technologies, Stoneham, Mass., http://www.circadian.com/. Light-level information from Ulrich Kraft, "Lighten Up," *Scientific American Mind*, Oct. 2005.

3:00 A.M.

A False Alarm: Adapted from Corey Binn, "A False Alarm," *Scientific American Mind,* Feb.–Mar. 2008. William Allstetter, "Panic Attacks and 'Suffocation Alarm Systems,'" *Journal of the College of Physicians and Surgeons of Columbia University,* 1999, *19*(1).

Dopamine, the Chemical of Delight, May Fuel Dread: Adapted from Adam Hadhazy, "Fear Factor: Dopamine May Fuel Dread, Too," *Scientific American Online,* July 14, 2008, http://www.sciam.com/article.cfm?id=fear-factor-dopamine.

That Pill to Fix Your Ills Has a Price: Adapted from Hal Arkowitz and Scott O. Lilienfeld, "A Pill to Fix Your Ills," *Scientific American Mind,* Feb.–Mar. 2007.

Night Nurse on Duty: Adapted from Ulrich Kraft, "Rhythm and Blues," *Scientific American Mind,* June–July 2007.

Background information: Anxiety Disorders Association of America, "Statistics and Facts About Anxiety Disorders," Mar. 2009, http://www.adaa.org/AboutADAA/PressRoom/Stats&Facts.asp. Rüdiger Vaas, "Fear Not," *Scientific American Mind,* Jan. 2004.

4:00 A.M.

Awake So Early? Adapted from J. R. Minkel, "Cellular Trafficking Could Explain Rare Morning Lark Syndrome," *Scientific American Online,* Sept. 19, 2006, http://www.sciam.com/search/index.cfm?q=CELLULAR+TRAFFICKING&submit.x=0&submit.y=0&submit=submit.

Illustration Credits

Clocks in the Brain: From Karen Wright, "Times of Our Lives," *Scientific American Special Edition,* June 2004. Artist: Terese Winslow.

Gateway to Consciousness and Emotions and Memory: From Gerhard Roth, "The Quest to Find Consciousness," *Scientific American Special Edition,* Jan. 2004. Artist: Carol Donner.

Structures for Seeing: From Nikos K. Logothetis, "Vision: A Window into Consciousness," *Scientific American Special Edition,* Sept. 2006. Artist: Terese Winslow.

A Cerebral Spot for Faces: From Nina Bublitz, "A Face in the Crowd," *Scientific American Mind,* Apr.-May 2008. Artist: SIGANIM.

The Vicious Cycle of Stress: From Robert M. Sapolsky, "Stressed Out Memories," *Scientific American Mind,* Dec. 2004. Artist: Alfred T. Kamajian.

Sensory Homunculus: From Chip Walter, "Affairs of the Lips," *Scientific American Mind,* Feb.-Mar. 2008. Artist: SIGANIM.

Feeling the Pain: From Allan I. Basbaum and David Julius, "Toward Better Pain Control." *Scientific American,* June 2006. Artist: Amadeo Bachar.

The Fear Response: From Marc Siegel, "Can We Cure Fear?" *Scientific American Mind,* Dec. 2005. Artist: Roberto Osti.

Singing in the Brain: From Norman M. Weinberger, "Music and the Brain," *Scientific American Special Edition,* Sept. 2006. Artist: Andrew Swift.

Mental Choreography and The Brain's Moving Parts: From Steven Brown and Lawrence M. Parsons, "The Neuroscience of Dance," *Scientific American*, July 2008. Artist: Tami Tolpa.

Anatomy of Aggression: From Daniel Strueber, Monika Lueck, and Gerhard Roth, "The Violent Brain," *Scientific American Mind*, Dec. 2006–Jan. 2007. Artist: SIGANIM.

When the Cleaning Stops (Autophagy in Alzheimer's?): From Vojo Deretic and Daniel J. Klionsky, "How Cells Clean House," *Scientific American*, May 2008. Artist: Jen Christiansen.

Humor in the Brain: From Steve Ayan, "Laughing Matters," *Scientific American Mind*, Apr./May/June 2009. Artist: Gehirn & Geist/SIGANIM.

Glossary

acetylcholine—a neurotransmitter chemical that appears to regulate memory and controls skeletal and smooth muscle action in the peripheral nervous system.

adenosine—a neurochemical that is part of adenosine triphosphate (ATP). It's released with each ATP action, building up in the body and making you sleepy. When your body is asleep, adenosine levels dwindle, helping you awake. *See* adenosine triphosphate.

adenosine triphosphate (ATP)—the energy mechanism that fuels cell metabolism.

adrenaline—*see* epinephrine.

amygdala—sometimes called the "emotional brain," it's the survival-oriented brain part that regulates primitive emotions and the fight-or-flight syndrome.

amyloid plaques—deposits found in the spaces between nerve cells in the brain that are made of beta-amyloid and other materials; believed to contribute to Alzheimer's disease.

anterior cingulate—establishes and processes emotional memory, linking emotion with the remembrance of specific feelings, including those from use of addictive drugs.

Source: This information was complied with permission primarily from glossaries and other resources of the National Institutes of Health.

apoptosis—programmed cell death; a cellular suicide mechanism.

arcuate nucleus—a section in the hypothalamus that regulates appetite by monitoring blood levels of glucose, insulin, and the hormones ghrelin and leptin to see if the body has enough calories and nutrients.

autophagy—"self-eating" (from the Greek); a process by which the body removes damaged and dying cells.

axon—the long extension from a neuron that transmits outgoing signals to other cells.

beta-amyloid protein—a part of the amyloid precursor protein found in plaques, the insoluble deposits outside neurons.

caudate nucleus—a part of the basal ganglia involved in coordinating body movement, emotion, and motivation.

cerebellum—two peach-size mounds of folded tissue located at the top of the brain stem that control skilled, coordinated movement (such as returning a tennis serve) and are involved in some learning pathways.

cerebral cortex—the "thinking brain": the outer three millimeters of gray matter consisting of closely packed neurons that control many processes including perception, memory, reasoning, language, and the mysterious state of consciousness.

cerebrum—often used to refer to the entire brain. The largest part of your brain, it accounts for about two-thirds of the brain's mass. It's divided into two hemispheres (*see* corpus callosum); has four lobes that control most body functions, thoughts, and senses; and is crowned by the cerebral cortex.

cingulate cortex—the brain part situated between the limbic system and cerebral cortex that gives emotional color to our physical perceptions, including our perceptions of pain and error.

computed tomography (CT) scan—a diagnostic imaging procedure that uses special x-ray equipment and computers to create cross-sectional pictures of the body.

corpus callosum—a fibrous bundle of axons that connects the two hemispheres of the brain.

cortisol—a natural steroid hormone produced by the adrenal gland in response to stress; an anti-inflammatory.

dementia—a broad term referring to a decline in cognitive function to the extent that it interferes with daily life and activities.

dentate gyrus—a region in the hippocampus involved with memory and learning; linked to age-related memory decline.

dopamine—a neurotransmitter involved in behavior, motivation, and reward as well as movement, mood, attention, and learning. A key player in addiction.

dorsal horn—an area of the spinal cord where many nerve fibers from peripheral sensory receptors meet other ascending and descending nerve fibers. The gateway to pain perception.

endorphins—hormones that also act as neurotransmitters to reduce pain sensations and increase pleasure. Exercise is known to increase endorphin levels.

entorhinal cortex—an area deep within the brain where damage from Alzheimer's disease often begins.

epinephrine—also called adrenaline. Keeps you alert, balances blood pressure, and is released in response to stress. Norepinephrine (noradrenaline) is similar.

frontal lobe—the most recently evolved part of the brain and the last to develop in young adulthood, it contains the brain's top executive and is responsible for so-called higher functions, including thinking, planning, and verbal skills patterns.

functional magnetic resonance imaging (fMRI)—a type of MRI brain scan that can show physical changes in the brain (such as blood flow) in correlation with mental activities (such as thoughts or feelings) as they occur. *See also* magnetic resonance imaging.

fusiform face area (FFA)—a specific center in a section of the brain called the fusiform gyrus dedicated to identifying faces.

fusiform gyrus—a spindle-shaped area where the temporal lobes meet the occipital lobe; known to help process color information, word and number recognition, as well as recognizing faces, bodies, and objects.

gamma-aminobutyric acid (GABA)—an inhibitory neurotransmitter that helps keep your system in balance. It helps regulates anxiety.

ghrelin—a hormone produced in cells lining the stomach, it stimulates appetite.

hippocampus—a structure located deep within the brain that plays a major role in learning and memory and is involved in converting short-term to long-term memory.

hypocretin—a tiny brain molecule produced in the hypothalamus; a shortage of this substance is connected with narcolepsy.

hypothalamus—a structure in the brain under the thalamus that monitors activities such as body temperature and food intake, blood pressure, and other body functions.

insula—a section deep in the brain connected with social emotions.

leptin—a hormone mostly produced from fat tissue, it puts the brakes on appetite after you've eaten.

limbic system—a brain region that links the brain stem with the higher reasoning elements of the cerebral cortex; controls emotions, instinctive behavior, and the sense of smell.

locus coeruleus—an attention center and the brain's main source of norepinephrine; important in responding to new or abrupt stimulants and in understanding depression, panic disorder, and anxiety.

magnetic resonance imaging (MRI)—a diagnostic and research technique that uses magnetic fields to generate a computer image of internal structures in the body; particularly good for imaging the brain and soft tissues. *See also* functional magnetic resonance imaging (fMRI).

melatonin—a hormone that helps regulate sleep and is produced in reaction to darkness.

metabolism—all of the chemical processes that take place inside the body.

myelin—"white matter," a whitish, fatty insulating layer surrounding an axon that helps the axon rapidly transmit electrical messages from the cell body to the synapse.

neuroeconomics—studies how the brain makes decisions, evaluates risks and rewards, and interacts with others.

neuron—a nerve cell.

neurotransmitter—a chemical messenger between neurons. These substances are released by the axon on one neuron and excite or inhibit activity in a neighboring neuron.

nociceptors—specialized neurons that sit outside the central nervous system; they detect potentially harmful environmental events and send messages up the spinal cord to your brain.

nucleus accumbens—part of the brain's reward system, located in the limbic system, that processes information related to motivation and reward. Virtually all drugs of abuse act on the nucleus accumbens to reinforce drug taking.

occipital lobe—processes and routes visual data to other parts of the brain for identification and storage.

orbitofrontal cortex—cerebral cortex covering the underside of the fontal lobes located above the orbits of the eyes. Involved in making decisions and other cognitive processes.

oxytocin—a hormone and a neurotransmitter produced in the hypothalamus that stimulates birth contractions and breast milk production as well as feelings of love and trust.

parietal lobe—receives and processes sensory information from the body, including calculating the location and speed of objects.

plasticity—the ability of the brain to change through the formation or strengthening of connections between neurons in the brain.

positron emission tomography (PET)—an imaging technique using radioisotopes that allows researchers to observe and measure activity in different parts of the brain by monitoring blood flow and concentrations of substances such as oxygen and glucose, as well as other specific constituents of brain tissues.

reticular activating system (RAS)—part of the brainstem that controls alertness by receiving and sending sensory and other information via a net of fibers that project widely throughout the brain.

seasonal affective disorder (SAD)—a depressed state brought on in some people by dim light that raises melatonin levels, typically in winter months in northern climates.

SCN—*see* suprachiasmatic nucleus.

selective serotonin reuptake inhibitors (SSRI)—a class of antidepressants that acts by increasing serotonin levels. *See* serotonin.

serotonin—a neurotransmitter that helps regulate body temperature, memory, emotion, sleep, appetite, and mood.

suprachiasmatic nucleus (SCN)—two tiny neuron groups in the hypothalamus important for maintaining circadian rhythms, especially for waking up.

synapse—the tiny gap between neurons across which neurotransmitters and electrical impulses pass.

tau protein—a key player in the development of Alzheimer's disease. Healthy tau supports neuron activity; modified tau is believed to contribute to brain tangles associated with Alzheimer's disease.

temporal lobe—controls memory storage area, emotion, hearing, and, on the left side, language.

temporoparietal junction—sits between the temporal lobes (involved in speech, memory, and hearing) and the parietal lobes (which integrate sensory input) and is activated when we think about others intentions and thoughts.

testosterone—the principal male hormone; responsible for the sex drive and aggression.

thalamus—located at the top of the brain stem. Acts as a relay station, sorting, processing, and directing signals to and from the spinal cord and midbrain structures up to the cerebrum, and down to the nervous system.

transcranial magnetic stimulation (TMS)—applying mild electrical current to the outside of the brain to stimulate activity and treat some conditions such as depression.

ventral tegmental area (VTA)—located in the midbrain at the top of the brain stem, the VTA is one of the most primitive parts of the brain. It synthesizes dopamine, which is sent to the nucleus accumbens.

ventromedial prefrontal cortex (VMPFC)—part of the prefrontal cortex, believed to have a role in the processing of risk and fear and in decision making.

About the Author

Judith Horstman is an award-winning journalist who writes about health and medicine for doctors as well as the general public. Her work has appeared in hundreds of publications worldwide and on the Internet.

The recipient of a Knight Science Journalism Fellowship at MIT, she was a journalism professor at Oregon State University and was later awarded two Fulbright Scholar grants to establish a center to teach fact-based journalism in Budapest, Hungary.

For several years, she edited a Web site for researchers and physicians on amyotrophic lateral sclerosis (also known as Lou Gehrig's disease), and she has written for the Stanford University Medical Center, the *Harvard Health Letter*, the Johns Hopkins University White Papers, and Time Inc. Health publications and she was a contributing editor for *Arthritis Today*, the magazine of the Arthritis Foundation. She has been a Washington correspondent for the Gannett News Service and *USA Today*, where her work included articles on medicine and health policy.

Horstman is the author of *The Arthritis Foundation's Guide to Alternative Therapies* and *Overcoming Arthritis* (with Dr. Paul Lam) and serves on the Medical Advisory Board for DxLupus.org.

About *Scientific American*

Scientific American is the world's leading source and authority for science and technology information. Since 1845, its magazines have chronicled the world's major science and technology innovations and discoveries. Published in nineteen foreign language editions with a total circulation of more than 1 million worldwide, *Scientific American* reaches business executives, opinion leaders, policymakers, academics, and well-educated general consumers. *Scientific American* is also a leading online science, health, and technology destination (www .SciAm.com), providing the latest news and exclusive features to more than 1.7 million visitors monthly and distributing its content through podcasts and other digital services.

Index